THE
TANGLED
GARDEN

A Canadian Cultural Manifesto
for the Digital Age

THE
TANGLED
GARDEN

A Canadian Cultural Manifesto
for the Digital Age

Richard Stursberg
With Stephen Armstrong

James Lorimer & Company Ltd., Publishers
Toronto

This book is dedicated to Clement.

James Lorimer & Company Ltd., Publishers acknowledges funding support from the Ontario Arts Council (OAC), an agency of the Government of Ontario. We acknowledge the support of the Canada Council for the Arts, which last year invested $153 million to bring the arts to Canadians throughout the country. This project has been made possible in part by the Government of Canada and with the support of Ontario Creates.

Cover design: Tyler Cleroux
Cover image: Vecteezy.com

Cover note: *The Tangled Garden* was painted by J.E.H. MacDonald, one of the Group of Seven. It was first exhibited at the Ottawa Society of Artists in March, 1916. It was derided. The art critic, Hector Charlesworth accused MacDonald of "throwing his paint pots in the face of the public." It remained unsold for twenty years. It is now one of the most admired paintings in the collection of the National Gallery.

Library and Archives Canada Cataloguing in Publication

Title: The tangled garden : a Canadian cultural manifesto for the digital age / Richard Stursberg with Stephen Armstrong.
Names: Stursberg, Richard (Richard Barclay), 1947- author. | Armstrong, Stephen, 1954- author.
Description: Includes bibliographical references and index.
Identifiers: Canadiana (print) 20190049464 | Canadiana (ebook) 20190049537 | ISBN 9781459413283 (softcover) | ISBN 9781459413290 (EPUB)
Subjects: LCSH: Cultural industries—Canada. | LCSH: Popular culture—Canada. | LCSH: Mass media—Canada. | LCSH: Canada—Cultural policy.
Classification: LCC HD9999.C9473 C3 2019 | DDC 338.4/73060971—dc23

James Lorimer & Company Ltd., Publishers
117 Peter Street, Suite 304
Toronto, ON, Canada
M5V 0M3
www.lorimer.ca

Printed and bound in Canada.

CONTENTS

Introduction 7

1 The Current Crisis 17

2 Creating the Garden 41

3 Expanding the Garden:
The Mulroney Years 59

4 Watering the Garden:
The Chrétien Liberals 95

5 The Garden Invaded:
The Harper Years 109

6 The Sleepy Gardeners:
The Justin Trudeau Years 139

7 The Manifesto 161

Conclusion 189

Acknowledgements 195

Notes 197

Index 221

INTRODUCTION

Living next door to the United States, the wealthiest and most dynamic country of the last hundred years, English Canada has always found it difficult to carve out a space for its own distinctive culture. It has been continually swamped with American TV, news, films, books and magazines, along with the values, hopes and dreams that they embody. No other country has lived in such close proximity to so powerful and overwhelming a neighbour with whom it shares both language and a commitment to freedom of expression.

The fear of being assimilated into the United States runs through the history of Canada's cultural, artistic and political life. The American embrace — both desired and reviled — is the fundamental existential threat. English Canada lives with the apprehension that it could vanish as a separate place, no more distinct than Ohio or Minnesota, swallowed up in the all-consuming pressure of Manifest Destiny.

In the mid-1960s, the political philosopher George Grant wrote *Lament for a Nation*, a despairing analysis of the impossibility of a separate Canada. In it, he quotes the great threnody from *Lucia di Lammermoor*: "I cannot but remember such things were that were most precious to me."[1] For

Grant, those most precious things were the values and way of life that distinguish Canada from the United States.

The most precious things are, indeed, Canada's different hopes and dreams, its different attitudes and beliefs, its different ties and bonds. It is the mutual understandings that exist among Canadians, the shared gossip, stories and laughter, the knowing wink, the self-deprecation and humble manners. It is the sum of these that make up the most precious things, the identity of the country as a separate people — clever, funny, worthy and different from the United States.

There are things we know in English Canada that will never be known to Americans: Don Cherry on Coach's Corner, "Four Strong Winds," the Six, the death of Gord Downie, *Little Mosque on the Prairie*, Sir John A., *Bon Cop, Bad Cop*, Stompin' Tom Connors, Truth and Reconciliation, the Rocket, We the North, Passchendaele, *Degrassi*, Sorry (both as a greeting and Justin Bieber's great hit), Tim Hortons, Tom Thomson, *The Handmaid's Tale*, vinegar on french fries, Buffy Sainte-Marie, burning down the White House, Dief the Chief, *Trailer Park Boys*, poutine, and on and on . . .

A real country, any real country, has stories, people, food, historical events and songs that are the touchpoints of its understanding of itself. They are the currency of mutual understanding — instantly recognized, a shorthand to a shared intimacy, like a secret national handshake. When the double-doubles are ordered and the dancing moose appear, everyone knows that they are home.

Cultures, like life itself, are continuously growing into the common dreams of the present and the shared hopes of the future. The soil in which they grow is the media:

the books, films, songs, magazines, newscasts and TV shows that make it all visible and accessible. It is through the mass media that the bonds of inside jokes, repeated stories and ubiquitous ideas are built. It is through them that national cultures are forged and a people's sense of itself is formed.

Canadian governments have always known that if there was to be a Canada, there would have to be Canadian media. Since the 1930s, successive administrations, whether Liberal or Conservative, have struggled to strengthen the foundations of Canadian culture, often in opposition to the desires of the United States. They passed laws, created regulations and provided financial support so that Canadian music, books, films, newspapers and TV shows could flourish. For almost 100 years, they worked — sometimes at significant political cost — to build counterweights to the great centripetal force of the US.

The most striking aspect of these efforts was its bipartisan character. The governments of Robert Borden, William Lyon Mackenzie King, Louis St. Laurent, John Diefenbaker, Pierre Trudeau, Brian Mulroney and Jean Chrétien all agreed that if there was to be a Canada, there had to be financially healthy media to ensure that Canada's distinctive culture prospered. While there may have been disagreement about means, there was always complete agreement on the end goal.

The effect of these efforts was, in many cases, simply to release the enormous pools of talent that were already in the country. The famous radio content quotas of the late 1960s and early 1970s did not create the Canadian music industry. Rather, what they did was to show the country the vast number of Canadian artists of world-class quality. The likes of Leonard Cohen, Joni Mitchell, Neil Young and The Band were succeeded over time by Alanis Morissette, The Tragically Hip, Justin Bieber, Drake and Arcade Fire. The country was — and has remained — a hotbed of musical talent.

Something similar could be seen in literature. The Canada Council's moves to support fiction also coincided with an explosion of internationally famous writers. The generation of Mordecai Richler, Margaret Atwood, Michael Ondaatje and Alice Munro swept up many of the world's top literary prizes, including the Nobel (Munro) and the Golden Man Booker (Ondaatje). They have been joined by more Booker winners and nominees, the likes of Yann Martel, Patrick deWitt, Esi Edgyan and Madeleine Thien.

Artistic success at these levels was not only important in its own right, it also served to make clear that Canadians could produce works that rivalled the quality of those produced anywhere in the world. It served to remind Canadians that despite their natural modesty, they were capable of achieving greatness. Canada was not some small and insignificant place, but a nation that nurtured excellence and brilliance.

By the turn of the millennium, this vast bipartisan national undertaking had borne reasonably impressive fruit. The newspaper business was flourishing; Canadian musicians, bands and songwriters were internationally famous; the Canadian TV industry counted dozens of channels and billions of dollars in production; even the notoriously underperforming Canadian movie business would, thanks to its Québécois wing, occasionally produce a hit and win an Oscar for best foreign-language film. With the growth of these businesses and the mirrors they created for Canadians to see themselves in, the confidence of the country surged, albeit in a quiet, self-effacing way.

Beginning around 2010, however, much of what had been accomplished began to erode. The emergence of the new US-based digital platforms of Facebook, Apple, Amazon, Netflix and Google (the FAANGs) began to compromise the financial viability of Canadian media businesses. Where, in the past, Canadian companies had spent their advertising dollars with Canadian magazines, newspapers and television networks, now they increasingly favoured Facebook and Google. Their money no longer stayed in Canada to support the creation of Canadian news and TV shows; it now flowed out of the country into the coffers of Silicon Valley.

The emergence of Netflix and Amazon dealt a second blow to the television industry. They entered the Canadian market unregulated, bearing none of the burdens shouldered by their Canadian counterparts. They did not collect or pay tax; nor did they have to contribute to the creation of Canadian TV shows or respect the country's broadcast standards rules.

The impact of the new digital platforms could not have been more dramatic. The once mighty newspaper industry struggled to survive, shedding journalists and closing bureaus across the country. The vastly profitable television business began to lose money. CTV, Global and Citytv, the powerhouses of the private news business and the biggest commissioners of Canadian drama and comedy, were all under water by 2012. The magazine and film businesses were also swept into the downdrafts created by the FAANGs.

As the crisis deepened, the Conservative government of Stephen Harper paid little attention. Indeed, to the extent that it addressed cultural questions at all, it was only to exacerbate the problems faced by Canadian media businesses. Rather than providing assistance, the Harper government went out of its way to help the foreign FAANGs and their hollowing-out of the Canadian cultural ecosystem.

When the Liberals returned to power in 2015, great hopes were expressed that they would address the peril facing the country. Strangely, however, they seemed gripped by a terrible lassitude. For the first three years of their mandate, they watched unmoved as news businesses collapsed and the FAANGs grew bolder and bolder. The Liberals seemed to be under Harper's spell, incapable of taking any action to address the existential threat to the country.

The FAANGs not only undermined Canadian media, they also brought with them a host of corrosive cultural influences. Fake news and hoaxes began crowding out true news; Facebook was weaponized to exacerbate ethnic tensions and filter bubbles; Canadian children were increasingly subjected to online bullying and harassment; privacy was constantly breached; and Canadians' personal data were shared with unethical marketers and political manipulators.

In Europe, the United States and the rest of the industrialized world, the behaviour of the FAANGs has been the subject of considerable study and concern. Parliamentary and Congressional hearings have taken place, massive studies have been undertaken, huge fines have been levied and new taxes have been imposed. The Europeans have implemented tough new legislation on hate speech and drafted laws requiring the FAANGs to contribute to the financing and distribution of European audio-visual content.

Despite the actions taken around the world and the imperilled state of Canadian media businesses, as of 2019, the Justin Trudeau government has remained on the sidelines, doing nothing. It has watched as the last century of nation-building unwound around it, as the great project of a North American, English-speaking alternative to the United States began to collapse.

The purpose of this book is to explain the breakdown of Canadian culture and to ask whether it can be salvaged from the embrace of the FAANGs. It examines in some detail how the current impasse arose and what — if anything — can be done about it.

It focusses on the largest of the media businesses — newspapers and television — and touches on film, magazines and books. It does not deal with music, except in passing, and has nothing to say about other important parts of our cultural life like the performing arts, libraries, galleries or museums. The core of the book is an exploration of the impact of new digital platforms on traditional media.

The book describes the bipartisan consensus that historically underpinned Canadian media and cultural policy, using as a metaphor the image of a garden. It shows how successive governments from the 1930s onward created a cultural garden in Canada, separate from the media ecosystem of the United States. It describes the measures that were put in place to define the garden and the supports that were created to water and tend it.

It reviews how the garden became tangled by the entry of the FAANGs, which appeared as invasive plants not unlike Japanese knotweed or dog-strangling vine. It explains how the invasive species began to crowd out the native species that had been cultivated for so many years. The book describes how the garden began to wither, how the flowers in it became bent and stooped.

The book is written from the point of view of a cultural nationalist. Almost all my adult life has been spent in the media trenches, wrestling with the problem of how to maintain a distinctive Canadian culture while living next door to the most dynamic country in the world.

In the 1980s, I worked as a public servant in the federal Department of Communications. As assistant deputy minister, I wrote, argued and worked on ways of extending and reinforcing the garden. I saw first-hand how important ministers and the Canadian cabinet struggled to resist the claustrophobic embrace of Uncle Sam.

Later, in the 1990s and 2000s, I was fortunate enough to be handed the reins at several of Canada's most important cultural companies and institutions. During the latter half of the 1990s, I was president of the Canadian Cable Television Association, where we worked hard both to launch new Canadian TV channels and to resist the entry of American direct-to-home satellite services, the so-called Death Stars, that would have unwound control of the Canadian television distribution system.

During the same period, I chaired the Canadian Television Fund (now the Canada Media Fund), an organization jointly created by the cable TV industry and the federal government, whose purpose was to finance the creation of Canadian television programs. We focussed not just on growing the financial resources available for production, but also on seeing that the shows that were financed were distinctly Canadian, that they spoke directly to Canadians, reflecting our landscapes, histories, stories and sensibilities.

In the early 2000s, I ran Telefilm Canada, the federal government's film financing agency. Gaining success for Canadian movies has always been much more daunting

— for reasons that will be discussed later — than for Canadian TV shows. While there, I tried hard, with mixed success, to ensure that the films we financed were both genuinely Canadian in character and also well received at the box office.

From there, I moved to CBC/Radio-Canada and became responsible for all the English services: TV channels (the main channel, the News Network and the Documentary channel); radio services (both Radio 1 and Radio 2); and online services (cbc.ca, podcasts and music streaming). It was an honour and an extraordinary challenge to run English Canada's most important cultural institution. (I wrote about the experience in some detail in my previous book, *The Tower of Babble*.)

Since leaving the corporation, I have continued to work on the problems of Canadian culture and media, sometimes writing about them and sometimes acting as a consultant. Over the last few years, my clients have included Torstar, the Canadian Media Producers Association, Rogers Communications Inc. and Rogers Media, Telefilm Canada and Postmedia. It has been sobering to see the impact of the FAANGs on these entities' businesses and their sometimes desperate struggles to cope with the changing environment.

The book, then, is written from the point-of-view of someone preoccupied by and immersed in all the various aspects of Canadian media and culture: films, television, newspapers, radio, music (a little), publishing (a little), magazines and digital content. It's the perspective of someone who believes in the importance of a strong and vibrant Canadian cultural ecosystem, who believes as well that time is running out to save English-Canadian culture from the great sea of Americana that floods our little garden. In my view, the current challenge to our traditional media is existential, with the future of Canada as a distinct country at stake.

The book summarizes what needs to be done. It lays out an agenda for action to save the great bipartisan effort that began in 1929 to preserve a distinct Canadian culture. It provides no guarantees of success, but points to a path that would certainly be more promising than the one the country is currently on. If action is taken soon, there is a chance to change the present trajectory of failure; if action is further delayed, there is little or no chance of saving English Canada from complete absorption into the US cultural ecosystem. Time is of the essence. She who dares, wins.

CHAPTER 1

The Current Crisis

On a bright day in November 2015, the new Liberal government of Justin Trudeau was sworn in by the governor general.

It was unseasonably warm, as though to mirror the new prime minister's "sunny ways."

He looked terrific, dressed in a slim blue suit, smiling his hundred-kilowatt smile and flashing his expertly tousled hair. He was accompanied by his beautiful wife, Sophie Grégoire, a former entertainment reporter and TV host. Their three small children scrambled along beside them, occasionally being picked up and carried by one of their parents.

The new prime minister had opened the gates of Rideau Hall to the Canadian public, so that ordinary citizens could participate in the ceremony. Large screens had been installed outside to allow them to see the swearing-in as it took place inside the mansion.

It was a marked contrast in tone and substance to the outgoing government of Stephen Harper. Where the Harper ministers arrived separately at Rideau Hall, the new Liberal cabinet arrived together in a bus. They walked up the driveway together, pausing occasionally to talk to the people lining the route. The prime minister shook hands and had selfies taken with anyone who asked.

Where the Tories had appeared sour and cramped, the Liberals had campaigned on warmth and openness.

The prime minister himself, only forty-four years old, seemed to symbolize a change not just in style, but in generations. He smiled constantly, shaking hands and opening his arms to everyone around him.

Where the Tories had appeared almost uniformly white and male, the Liberal ministers were half women and many wore turbans. The new minister of justice was a Kwakwaka'wakww woman from British Columbia.

They were a much more diverse and younger group than the one they succeeded.

They were, as well, a group that was clearly hipper and more urban. They were international in outlook, committed to racial and sexual equality and technologically sophisticated. To emphasize their modernity, the prime minister had the entire ceremony streamed live through Periscope on his Twitter feed.

They were also committed to strengthening Canada's culture.

Where Stephen Harper had sneered at the "cultural elites" and cut funding to the CBC, Telefilm and the Canada Council, the new government promised to undo the cuts and bring a bright new approach.

Emblematic of the change in both style and substance was the incoming minister of Canadian heritage — effectively the minister of culture — Mélanie Joly. Only thirty-six years old, photogenic and fashionably dressed, she was the poster child for the new-look Liberals.

Her career had been remarkable. She had received her

law degree (honours) when she was twenty-two, and joined the well-connected firm of Stikeman Elliott, where she was mentored by Lucien Bouchard, the onetime great friend and later separatist enemy of Brian Mulroney.

While there, she won the Chevening Scholarship. It was offered by the British government for people it believed would be "future leaders in their countries." Previous winners had included the chief justice of Sri Lanka, the prime ministers of Poland, Iceland, Antigua and Bulgaria, along with the president of Colombia. The scholarship had taken her to Oxford, where she earned a Master of Laws (Magister Juris).

She had run for the mayoralty of Montreal at the age of thirty-four under the banner "Vrai Changement pour Montreal." Although a political neophyte, she came within six points of beating Denis Coderre, a seasoned Liberal operator who had been a federal cabinet minister.

In Joly's mandate letter, the prime minister had spelled out a long list of things that she needed to do to repair the great institutions of Canadian culture. She was to "restore and increase funding for CBC/Radio-Canada, Telefilm and the National Film Board (NFB)." She was, as well, to "double investment in the Canada Council for the Arts." She was also to "make significant investments in cultural infrastructure."

Almost immediately after taking office, Joly made good on the Liberals' promises to restore funding to the big cultural agencies. Money poured into the CBC, the NFB and the others.

Bliss was it in that dawn to be the Canadian minister of culture.

It was hard to imagine then that everything would fall apart so quickly for the new minister.

It was hard to imagine, but the problems were already implicit in her mandate letter — not in what was said, but in what was left unsaid.

There was no mention of the radical shift in media consumption. By the time the new cabinet was sworn in, everyone under the age of fifty-five was spending more time online than watching TV.[1] The traditional Canadian media diet of newspapers, magazines and television shows was being replaced by Facebook, Apple, Amazon, Netflix and Google. Of the top twenty-five websites in Canada, almost every one of them was based in the United States. Canada had virtually no presence in the online diet of Canadians.[2]

There was no mention, as well, of the continuing erosion of the advertising markets that had crushed the finances of newspapers and conventional television, leaving them gasping for breath. At the time of Joly's appointment, almost 40 per cent of Canada's advertising revenue had fled to the new digital platforms, with the vast majority of those revenues going to Google and Facebook, leaving the country to finance the creation of algorithms in California.[3]

There was nothing, as well, about the increasingly malign influence the new platforms were having on everything from the promulgation of fake news and the invasion of privacy to the destruction of legacy media and the corrosion of democracy. There was nothing about the extent to which they were coarsening civic discourse or widening cleavages within society.

Nor was there any mention of the impact that Netflix was having on the broadcasting system. Millions of Canadians had already subscribed to the service[4] and many of them, especially in English Canada, had begun cutting the cords that bound them to their cable and satellite subscriptions, stepping away from Canadian TV altogether.[5]

There was no sense that the big media companies — the giant newspaper chains and the major networks, the most important parts of the Canadian cultural ecosystem — faced imminent collapse. Newspaper and magazine operating revenues were in free fall.[6] The TV networks had been losing money for at least three years before the new government took power.[7]

There was no understanding that when the newspapers and magazines failed, they had knock-on effects on other media. As their book review sections dwindled and their film critics were laid off, Canadians had less and less information about what to read or see. They did not know whether new books had been published, let alone whether they were worth reading. The media constitute an interconnected ecosystem; problems for one section often translate into problems for all.

Finally, there was no sense that as Canadian media eroded and Canadians embraced the new foreign, digital platforms, they walked away from Canada itself. They no longer consumed Canadian news, laughed at Canadian comedies, watched Canadian documentaries or read the opinions of Canadian experts on domestic social, cultural, political or economic issues. They effectively left the national conversation and moved to another amorphous, filter-bubbling virtual country.

The mandate letter was wholly backward looking. For a government that prided itself on being digitally sophisticated, it seemed not to have heard about the dramatic and convulsive changes that were sweeping the Canadian cultural sector. The letter could have been composed fifty years earlier.

In April 2016, the minister, appearing to understand that putting more money into the CBC and the Canada Council was not enough to deal with the challenges at hand, announced a review of Canadian cultural policy. It was to cover TV, radio, film, digital media and platforms, video games, books, newspapers and magazines.

Joly seemed ideally suited to carry out such a review. Brilliantly educated, politically savvy, she appeared the ideal emissary to the cultural community. She was also a self-styled "digital native," at home with the technological changes that were transforming the industries.

According to the minister, "Everything was on the table."

She said, "the current model is broken, and we need to have a conversation to bring it up to date and make sure we harness its full potential. For a long time, politicians have been afraid to deal with these difficult issues, but I don't understand why it wasn't done . . . The issue is how the government can be relevant today, instead of being left behind."[8]

If there was ever a time for a big review of Canadian cultural policy, it was in 2016. If there was ever a time to reaffirm the importance of Canadians being able to "tell their own stories," it was when they were increasingly spending their leisure hours with the glittering new stories of YouTube, Netflix and Amazon Prime.

For the next eighteen months, the minister held consultations.

In keeping with the "digital" emphasis of the review, she set up #DigiCanCon and various other social media sites for input and discussion with the public.

She established groups of experts to advise her, and had meetings across the country. Some of these produced slightly odd conversations. Ballet dancers and actors were thrown together with media executives to discuss what to do, yielding strange, but sometimes arresting ideas.

As the meetings were going on, the minister encouraged Canadians to set up their own forums to discuss the future of Canadian culture. She created an online toolkit to show them how to proceed. She asked that they submit their recommendations to a website created for the purpose.

To ensure that the national debate was properly framed, she gave pep talks on the importance of culture. She explained the centrality of culture to the economy in speeches to business groups across the country. "It is a big business," she would say, showing charts and graphs to prove it.

And she was right: Culture is an enormous business in Canada. It is worth, by the government's reckoning, almost $54 billion per year and employs 650,000 people.[9] This makes it almost twice as large as the agriculture, forestry and fisheries industries combined. It accounts for double the number of jobs in mining and oil and gas.[10]

In the summer of 2017, Joly appeared at the Banff World Media Festival, an annual gathering of the great and the good in the TV business, to explain to somewhat bewildered executives that — just as they had believed all their lives — culture was big business, the future was "digital" and that they needed to take "risks."

In a restless flurry of meetings across North America, Joly carried her "digital/big business/take risks" message to all and sundry. She met with favour-seekers, performing artists, Silicon Valley tycoons, cultural mavens of one variety or another and young entrepreneurs. She was working very hard to move the discussion forward.

While her consultations were proceeding, a number of large studies and reports were released.

The first of these was commissioned by Rogers Communications Inc., Canada's second-largest integrated media company. It was commissioned as a contribution to the minister's review of cultural policy. Entitled *Cultural Policy for the Digital Age*, it was released publicly in late 2016 at a seminar at the law school of the University of Ottawa. (Full disclosure: It was written by me.)

The paper provided a detailed economic analysis of the problems facing Canadian media businesses and projections of the likely consequences of inaction by the government. It proposed a series of measures to rectify the problems. These involved putting the FAANGs on the same footing in Canada as their Canadian competitors and providing subsidies to news operations in the same way that subsidies are provided to television production. It costed the proposals and showed how they might be implemented without imposing new taxes or further draws on the national treasury.[11]

The next major study appeared in early 2017, in the form of a report on the state of the newspaper industry by the Public Policy Forum, one of Canada's oldest and most distinguished think tanks.

The Shattered Mirror: News, Democracy and Trust in the Digital Age was the largest and most comprehensive report on the state of the Canadian news business since the 1970s. More than three hundred people were consulted, extensive studies were undertaken and roundtables were held with experts across the country.

The report had been commissioned and financed in part by the Canadian government.

In language that was much more apocalyptic than *Cultural Policy for the Digital Age*, it warned that "Real news is in crisis." Canadians, it noted "need — and want — real news to make educated decisions about their governments and keep the powerful accountable. Without it, we'll be in the dark about our communities and our country. Without it, democracy itself is at risk."[12]

The Shattered Mirror described the same financial pressures that were reviewed in *Cultural Policy for the Digital Age*. "Established news organisations have been left gasping," it said. "The financial degradation has been insidiously incremental, but one whose accumulation and now acceleration has brought to the fore the issue of the sustainability of news gathering in our democracy."[13]

The report cited a famous observation made by Thomas Jefferson about the relationship between news and democracy. When asked if he had to choose between government without newspapers or newspapers without government, he said, "I should not hesitate a moment to prefer the latter."[14] So central is accurate news to the functioning of a democracy that it is hard to imagine good government without it.

The Public Policy Forum urged the government to act. It proposed a number of measures to save the news business and safeguard Canadian democracy. The first and most important of these was a Future of Democracy and Journalism Fund. "Its role would be to support . . . digital news innovation and . . . civic function journalism."[15]

The Shattered Mirror was followed by the Standing Committee on Canadian Heritage's report, *Disruption: Change and Churning in Canada's Media Landscape*. The committee expressed dismay at how difficult the situation

had become for the country's most important media businesses. It reviewed the collapse of the Canadian advertising
market and the steady draining of revenues into the United
States. It warned that, as a result, both the newspaper and
broadcasting industries were in a perilous state.

It noted, like the others, that the fourth estate was an
essential part of the country's life. The report said: "The
importance of reporting on local institutions and local democracy cannot be overstated; without it, there is little democratic
accountability."[16] It, too, proposed the creation of support
mechanisms for the newspaper business and simply recommended that "the Government of Canada introduce a tax
credit to compensate print media companies for a portion of
their capital and labour investments in digital media."

The standing committee's report, unlike the other two,
was produced by a committee of the House of Commons,
with Hedy Fry, a former Liberal cabinet minister, chairing it
and a majority of its members coming from the new government's backbenches. It was assumed that the committee
would not make recommendations that would be inconsistent with the government's plans.

All the studies made the point that Canadian public life
— like that of much of the rest of the Western world —
was increasingly compromised by the plague of fake news
designed to sow suspicion, distrust and anger. Fake news had
played on American fears in the 2016 election, with polariz-
ing results. In Canada, fake stories about Muslims had begun
to circulate. The clearest solution to the problem was true
news based on objective reporting and traditional journalistic standards of accuracy.

Since all the studies — coming from very different
sources — agreed on the problem and proposed a number

of similar approaches to dealing with it, the government and the industry looked to be in a good position to define a new cultural policy and move ahead.

By the summer of 2017, the minister had a wealth of information and consultations out of which to fashion her new cultural policy. By Joly's own count, more than 30,000 Canadians had participated in her review, whether by attending meetings, filing proposals or organizing their own conversations.

The results of all this work had been widely anticipated for some time. There had been a general feeling that the minister's review had gone on a little too long and that it was past time for her to show her hand. Finally, after eighteen months of work, the minister unveiled her *Creative Canada Policy Framework*. Glossy papers in both official languages were released to the waiting country.[17]

The initial reaction to the framework was surprise. It appeared that when the minister finally had something to say, it was almost nothing. The framework hardly touched on any of the subjects she said were on the table. There was nothing about newspapers, books, TV, radio, film, computer games or magazines.

Instead, Joly announced again the money that had already been given to the CBC, Telefilm, the Canada Council et al. She indicated that she would undertake a number of studies and reviews of everything from the operations of the magazine publishing support program to the *Broadcasting Act*. She even put a little new money into supporting the export of Canadian cultural goods.

But there was nothing in the framework to address, let alone resolve, the issues raised by the major studies. There was no discussion of the erosion of the advertising markets, the problems of the newspaper and TV industries or the roles of the new US-based digital platforms. The contributions of Rogers, the Public Policy Forum and the standing committee were completely ignored.

The minister did not mention the ongoing collapse of Canada's biggest media companies. It seemed that she did not understand that a major hollowing-out was taking place of the country's intellectual and cultural life. She seemed not to understand what was at stake; she seemed, in fact, not to care.

Instead of dealing with the fallout from the FAANGs' operations in Canada, Joly made announcements about deals she had made with them. The two companies that had done most to erode the Canadian news business had agreed to set up initiatives to help.

Google was putting $500,000 into a media literacy initiative to help ensure that school children could distinguish between real and fake news. Even the most hardened and jaded commentators were taken aback.

Equally bizarrely, the minister announced that Facebook would be investing $500,000 and working with Ryerson University to create a "digital news incubator."

Most notoriously, the centrepiece of the policy was an agreement that Netflix would invest $500 million over the next five years to produce TV shows in Canada. The details of the deal were not made public, but it appeared that Netflix would not necessarily be making Canadian TV shows.

The reaction to the framework was a mixture of rage and guffaws.

Joly was pilloried for making news deals with the very companies that were responsible for the collapse of the news industry.

She was criticized for advantaging foreign television firms over Canadian ones by not requiring them to contribute to the support of Canadian culture or pay taxes.

And she was mocked for her naivety.

When experts recalculated her Netflix deal, they showed that she had been snookered. They pointed out that if Netflix had to play by the same rules as Canadian broadcasters, it would have had to produce $230 million worth of Canadian TV shows in the first year of the deal, with the number probably rising to more than $300 million in the last. Joly might have left almost a billion dollars on the table.[18]

In a catastrophic appearance on the popular French-language talk show, *Tout le monde en parle*, Joly was relentlessly attacked for favouring a foreign company at the expense of Canadian ones. The hosts mocked her for letting Netflix escape collecting sales tax. They pointed out that all the similar Canadian companies collected the tax. How, they asked, could she let a foreign company in Canada enjoy advantages not available to its Canadian competitors?

Joly responded by saying that "the government's policy is not to add additional taxes on the middle class. We promised Canadians that we would not tax Netflix because we do not want to add to the burden already being borne by ordinary Canadians."[19]

This provoked further jeers and anger. As the program wore on, she repeated — almost robotically — her lines about middle-class Canadians. She was accused over and over of not listening to or answering the question.

The next morning, her appearance and performance were declared a fiasco.

The *Globe and Mail* noted that "Her fall from grace in her home province has been swift and merciless, sped by her

maladroit attempts to sell a deal with Netflix that would give
the company a free pass from tax and regulation in exchange
for an ill-defined CanCon investment of $500 million over
five years. The minister has been roasted and ridiculed to her
face on live radio and TV, and dismissed by commentators
of all stripes as naïve and — worst of all — unable even to
understand what the fuss is about."[20]

In a little-noticed part of Joly's *Creative Canada Policy
Framework*, there appeared to be an oblique admission that
she had failed to master the major cultural problems facing
the country. She asked the Canadian Radio-television and
Telecommunications Commission (CRTC) to write a report
on all the problems that had been ignored by her policy
framework — and to report in nine months what she had not
been able to accomplish in eighteen.

Joly explained that the government was asking the CRTC
"to report . . . on future models for the distribution of
Canadian content and the extent to which these models will
ensure a vibrant domestic market capable of supporting the
continued creation, production and distribution of Canadian
programming . . ."[21]

The commission dutifully went about its work. It called
for comments and organized public proceedings to examine
the various issues.

As part of its efforts, the CRTC released a consultation paper, describing the key facts that everyone needed
to be aware of. It noted — as the earlier reports had — the
dramatic shift in advertising revenues to the coffers of the
FAANGs and the resulting loss of profitability of the big
conventional broadcasters.

All the usual suspects — the big Canadian television
networks, the industry's unions, the film and TV producers

and the cable and telephone companies — filed briefs. There was significant consensus on many points. Most importantly, they all wanted a "level playing field" for Netflix's operations in Canada. They wanted Netflix to pay the same taxes and make the same contributions to Canadian content as the Canadian broadcasters did.

A few months after the CRTC started its work, Finance Minister Bill Morneau began consultations on what should be in his third budget.

The media industries — and particularly the newspapers — lobbied vigorously for the government to throw them a lifeline and level the playing field with the FAANGs.

As the Public Policy Forum had noted, the newspaper industry had seen a precipitous decline over many years. Since 2008, almost 170 news outlets had been closed or merged,[22] where there had been more than one newspaper purchased by every household in Canada in 1950, there would be basically nobody buying them by 2022.[23]

As if to drive home how tough times were, at the end of 2017, Torstar and Postmedia, the country's two largest newspaper companies, swapped forty-one titles and then closed all but five of them, eliminating almost 300 jobs. The minister's reaction was curious. Instead of expressing sympathy for the problems of the industry, she denounced the newspapers and described the closures as "cynical business decisions." She asserted that "There are many media companies that have made a smooth transition [to digital] and have been able to innovate and be profitable."[24]

Aside from her failure to understand the implications of the collapse of the news business, her statement was false. Very, very few media companies had made "a smooth transition." The problems facing the news business in Canada were more or less the same all over the Western world. It was, in fact, extremely difficult to point to any companies that had made a "smooth transition."

For its part, the government, rather than seeing the closures as part of the broader structural crisis, sent in the Competition Bureau to investigate the matter and see whether charges should be laid and executives from the Post and the Star arrested.

Starting in the new year, however, the tone of the government seemed to change. The Prime Minister's Office began to make encouraging public noises and there was speculation that something would happen.

The Canadian Press reported that "The federal government is signalling the country's newspaper industry is set to get financial help, with the minister in charge [Joly] of the file vowing measures in this year's budget and officials ready to meet with publishers to talk details."[25]

The chairman of the newspaper lobby, News Media Canada, said, "we've had an indication from the prime minister's mouth and the minister's mouth that there will be help for newspapers . . ."[26]

There was less optimism, however, on the Netflix front.

After the debacle on *Tout le monde en parle*, Joly attempted to distance herself from the sales-tax controversy by pointing out that she was "in charge of culture. Mr. Morneau is Finance Minister and in charge of taxation."[27]

For his part, Morneau reiterated the government's stand that it had "no plans to introduce a Netflix tax of any kind, as it would be a financial hit to middle-class Canadians."[28]

When the budget was finally brought down in February 2018, it was a great disappointment. There was effectively nothing in it to address the concerns raised by the media companies. The FAANGs remained untaxed and there was no lifeline for the newspapers.

Minister Joly said again that she would not support failing business models. "Our approach will not be to bail out industry models that are no longer viable."[29]

A few months later, in May, the vastly wealthy, impeccably connected Desmarais family, seeing that the government would not do anything about the crisis gripping the newspaper industry, threw in the towel, abandoning *La Presse*. They announced that they were turning Quebec's largest and most influential newspaper into a not-for-profit trust. They would put up $50 million to endow it, but otherwise they would have nothing more to do with the paper the family had owned for fifty years.

The Desmarais family said that they — the richest family in Quebec, worth almost $10 billion — could no longer bear the losses. They said, as well, that creating the trust would free the government to provide subsidies directly to the paper. No government, they felt, could ever be seen to give money to billionaires.

This latter argument was odd. Other billionaire families — the Rogers (Citytv), the Shaws (Global) and the Péladeaus (TVA) — had received government subsidies for many years, in some cases decades. Like the CTV group and the CBC, their broadcasters had received millions in tax credits and Canada Media Fund money for the dramas, kids' shows and documentaries that they put on their TV networks. The government position had always been that the money was to make Canadian television economically viable. It was not money to billionaires. Why the Desmarais family felt that the same approach would not apply to newspapers was not clear.

Whatever the merits of the Desmarais family's approach,

it also looked like an opportunity foregone. When Jeff Bezos, the founder of Amazon, bought the *Washington Post*, he did so in the belief that when the news business finally shakes out, there will be a number of great international brands that survive. For this reason, he told the *Post* management not to worry about near-term profits, but to focus on getting as many subscribers as possible. Once the dust settled, they would figure out how to make money.

The Desmarais family, like Bezos, were uniquely positioned to turn *La Presse* into one of the international news brands that will survive in the future. With the exception of *Le Figaro* in Paris, there are no other major French papers in the world that have billionaire family owners. If they had been prepared to make the investments to build something great, they might have been able — like the Canadian news barons of old, like Max Aitken and Roy Thomson — to create an internationally competitive news empire.

The Desmarais family's approach is clearly not, however, a solution for Postmedia or Torstar. They are publicly traded companies with no big money backing them. If they are to survive, it will have to be on the basis of something other than turning themselves into charities, which would hold little interest for their shareholders.

The cold water that Mélanie Joly had thrown on the newspapers continued for Canadian media more generally. Despite the endless erosion of the advertising markets, the government did nothing to level the playing field. The FAANGs remained untaxed.

The prime minister, speaking in the House of Commons, said that the government "explicitly promised in the 2015 election campaign that we would not be raising taxes on Netflix. People may remember Stephen Harper's attack ads on that. They were false. We actually moved forward in demonstrating that we are not going to raise taxes on consumers, who pay enough for their internet at home."[30]

The government's position was very odd. Regardless of the unfairness of not taxing Netflix, regardless of the reaction in Quebec and the rest of the country, regardless of the destruction of the minister of heritage's credibility, it would not move. It was as though it was under remote control from the previous government.

Four months later, the CRTC handed in its report.[31] A strangely tentative document, *Harnessing Change: The Future of Programming Distribution in Canada* described the rise of the new digital media platforms and the perilous financial situation of the traditional broadcasting sector. It then went on to suggest that it might be a good idea to "ensure that all players benefitting from Canada and Canadians participate in an appropriate and equitable — though not necessarily identical — way to benefit Canada and Canadians." What form this "equitable" participation might take was never made clear. There was vague talk about entering into "agreements" with the new players, but no specifics on how it might be done.

More discouragingly, while the commission recognized it could use its existing powers to address the challenges in the broadcasting system, it did not actually undertake to do anything. It did not propose to force Netflix to contribute fairly to the production of Canadian content; nor did it undertake to assist the collapsing fortunes of the conventional broadcasters. Rather, it treated all of its ideas as mere proposals that the federal government might want to consider.

Minister Joly thanked the CRTC for its hard work and

referred its report to yet another committee, a Task Force on Legislation, to study its recommendations and see what changes to the law might be necessary. She asked the task force to report by the end of January 2020, more than a year and a half after she had received the commission's report. By pushing a decision past the 2019 election, she effectively guaranteed further government paralysis for at least another two years.

Having accomplished next to nothing and having outraged the cultural elites in Quebec, Mélanie Joly was shuffled out of the culture portfolio by the prime minister and demoted to minister of tourism. In her place, he named Pablo Rodriguez as the new minister of Canadian heritage. Curiously, he provided no new instructions to Rodriguez. A new mandate letter was provided six weeks later but it instructed him to stay the course by working with the Minister of Innovation, Science and Economic Development to continue work on the modernization of the *Broadcasting Act* and *Telecommunications Act*. The time line for the Task Force report remained January 2020.

Unlike Mélanie Joly, Pablo Rodriguez did not have a flashy résumé. He had a business degree and had worked as an administrator for an international charity. He had been elected in 2004 and spent the next fourteen years languishing on the back benches, save for 2011–2015, when his seat turned over to the NDP. There was little in his past to suggest that he had the background or experience to save Canada from the FAANGs. The government clearly had no appetite for major change, since it had already tied its own hands by setting up the new Task Force on Legislation.

Remarkably, however, Rodriguez showed himself a deft operator. He managed to get the government to reverse itself partially on one point and made some progress where Mélanie Joly had made none. In his November 2018 fall economic statement, Finance Minister Morneau announced a new program of financial support for the newspaper industry. Without specifying who would qualify or what types of content, he pledged $595 million over five years to be spent on a variety of customer subscription tax credits, labour tax credits and new charitable arrangements. The government appeared to have changed its mind about "bailing out failed business models." In fact, it appeared that the government was prepared to help the papers make the "digital transition."

The money was scheduled to begin flowing in 2019, but the pattern of the release was very peculiar. The bulk of the $595 million was back-end loaded. Only $45 million would be available in the first year, with increasing amounts available in each succeeding year to a maximum of $165 million in 2023. This was odd, because if the papers were really making the digital transition, their digital revenues would be growing year over year, reducing the need for a subsidy as time went by, not requiring more. What they needed instead was the larger amount of money right away to stem their losses, so that they could have enough cash to be able to arrive at the "transition." The whole structure of the program seemed upside down.

It was also clear that $45 million would not go very far in 2019. The newspaper industry's leading publishers, Postmedia and Torstar who together account for about half of the industry's revenues, had been losing enormous amounts of money over the last few years despite relentless cost-cutting. They were likely to lose at least $35 million in 2018 and more again in 2019. In fact, if the publishers' revenues fell in 2019 at the same pace as the preceding two years and they did not engage in even more radical slashing, Postmedia and Torstar were on a pace to lose almost $170 million.[32] The $45 million was, at best, a sop to the newspapers. It would not eliminate the need for further cuts nor revive any of the almost 200 newspapers that had already folded.

Finally, the new policy did nothing to level the playing field. Google and Facebook remained untaxed, never having to collect HST on their advertising sales. For their part, the newspapers would have to continue to do so, leaving them priced higher than their competitors.

Cynics suggested that the reason the government had structured the new money in such a peculiar and inadequate way was to discipline the newspapers during the 2019 electoral season. The implicit message was clear: If the papers wanted to qualify for the future larger amounts of money, they had to behave themselves. Make sure the Liberals return; the Tories might not be so generous.

Nevertheless, the industry made positive public noises, thanking the government and welcoming the new money. It reasoned, no doubt, that it would seem churlish to point out the program's shortcomings and unwise to bite the hand that feeds.

By the beginning of 2019, Canada's cultural policy was in tatters. The bipartisan consensus on its importance had evaporated with the arrival of the Harper Conservatives. And the Liberals, for their part, seemed neither to understand the issues involved nor to have any appetite to address them. Rather, the seventy-five-year history of cross-party consensus on the importance of a clear cultural strategy had arrived at a place where there appeared to be no strategy at all.

It wasn't just newspapers that were in dire straits. CTV,

Global and Citytv had all been losing money since 2012, in spite of furious cost-cutting. It looked, in fact, as though they might lose more than $170 million in 2018, rising to almost $300 million in 2020.[33] The government had not, however, done anything to help. It would not be surprising if the networks' owners decided that there was no point continuing to lose money and simply shut them down.

This, in fact, is what the Shaws, the controlling shareholders of Corus, seemed to have concluded. In late 2018, they put their position up for sale, offering up the second-largest collection of TV channels in Canada. Apart from Global, the group includes YTV, Teletoon, Treehouse, Slice and a host of other networks focussed on women and children. As of early 2019, no buyer had emerged.

So too, Rogers, decided that it no longer wanted to be in the magazine business. It tried to sell some of Canada's most iconic titles, including *Maclean's* and *Chatelaine*. Like the Shaws, Rogers had great trouble finding any buyers.

Thus, at the beginning of 2019, the situation was very dark. The biggest media companies seemed destined for insolvency and the government had no game plan. The danger for the Liberal government of Justin Trudeau and Pablo Rodriguez was that it was running out of time. Unless it changed direction very soon, it could end up presiding over the utter collapse of Canadian culture. Where they had promised a sea change from the dark days of Stephen Harper's endless bashing of the CBC and his withering scorn for artistic life, they could soon find themselves living in the arid and lifeless landscape of an abandoned culture.

CHAPTER 2
Creating the Garden

On a sunny day in 1929, Sir John Aird, the redoubtable president of the Canadian Bank of Commerce, handed the Liberal government of Mackenzie King the final report of the Royal Commission on Radio Broadcasting.

He was not an ordinary banker. He was eulogized at the time of his death as "The Grand Old Man of Canadian Finance" and, according to the *Montreal Gazette*, one of the twenty-one "real rulers" of the Dominion. He was a man of considerable heft and influence.

Aird was seventy-four years old. He was born in 1855, six years before the outbreak of the Civil War in the US and twelve years before Confederation. Portraits capture essentially a Victorian man, wing collared, well fed and confident.

He had grown up in a world without electronic media. There was no broadcasting of any variety in Canada until 1919 (when Marconi began in Montreal). By then, Aird was already sixty-four years old. The media world that he had been born into and knew in old age was one of books, church choirs, live theatre and newspapers.

Despite his limited familiarity with modern media, Aird's modest report — a mere twenty-six pages — provided the framework for the development of the Canadian broadcasting industry over the next eighty years. The application of his principles and ideas created the largest and most important part of the Canadian cultural ecosystem. It also set out the major challenges and policy approaches that would underpin Canadian cultural policy. His work anticipated the major themes that would preoccupy successive governments, whether about books, movies, TV, newspapers or radio.

Aird worried that: "At present, the majority of programs heard are from sources outside Canada. It has been emphasized to us that continued reception of these sources has a tendency to mould the minds of young people . . . to ideals and opinions that are not Canadian."[1]

Aird feared that endless exposure to American news and entertainment would ultimately turn young Canadians into little Americans.

This preoccupation about the potentially corrosive influence of the US on Canada's sense of itself has been the leitmotif of a debate that has continued for the ensuing ninety years. Aird's formulation was, in a nutshell, the fundamental challenge of Canadian cultural policy: How is it possible to have a country if the most popular cultural products its citizens consume come from another place?

Just a decade after the end of the First World War, Aird saw the problem with respect to the new medium of radio. As the years went by, all through the twentieth century, Canadians would ask themselves over and over again what to do about the American behemoth next door. The technology changed but the problem stayed the same. How does Canada build and maintain a distinct culture in the face of technology's tendency to overwhelm its border and bring with it the stories, news, songs, films and dreams of the US?

The problem of dealing with the US is different between French and English Canada. Quebec enjoys the insulation of language, which mitigates the American presence. Quebec's TV and film industries have always produced shows and movies that have connected with their home audiences. French Canada has also produced a star system (*la vedetterie*) so powerful that it has inspired hand-wringing among the political and intellectual elites about the scope and size of its influence.

English Canada, however, shares the same language and, in many cases, the same accents as the US, which makes it much more vulnerable. It has never been as successful as Quebec at producing popular cultural products, whether TV shows, books or movies. It has no star system; the celebrity magazines in the grocery stores are all about Americans.

The relative weakness of English Canada has resulted in a strangely ambivalent attitude to cultural policy. Sometimes it is seen as an urgent matter that involves profound challenges to the very idea of an independent country. At other times, it is seen as a hopeless task to try and build a distinctive culture next door to the elephant. The national mood on these matters has waxed and waned over the decades. As of early 2019 we still appear to be at a particularly passive time.

But whenever the debate occurs about Canadian culture — whether now, in the 1960s or before the Second World War — it always revolves around the major themes first explored by Aird.

To deal with the problem of US radio dominance and ensure the existence of Canadian services with Canadian content, Aird proposed a two-fold approach.

First, he recommended the creation of a "national company that will own all radio broadcasting stations

located in the Dominion of Canada."[2] His notion was that
the border was to be secured by ensuring that the means of
distribution were owned and controlled by Canadians. The
"means of distribution" for radio is, of course, the studios
and transmitters that are used to make radio shows available
to the public.

Aird's proposal was simple. Whatever radio programs
were made available to Canadians, the stations that distributed them would have to be Canadian. In the case of his
report, he recommended that the stations be owned by a
crown corporation, which would ultimately become the
CBC.

Second, that when foreign content — US radio shows —
came into Canada, they had to be distributed by Canadians.
This would not only help reinforce the border, it would also
allow the foreign shows to be used to assist the production
and promotion of Canadian ones. By buying the US shows
at prices that were significantly below what it would cost to
make domestic ones, the CBC could use them to underwrite
its more expensive Canadian fare.

In effect, Aird had proposed that Canadian media be insu-
lated within a sort of garden. The garden would not allow
foreign distributors in and would ensure that the foreign
content that entered could be used — in part, at least — as
fertilizer for the creation of Canadian content.

Thus, Aird enunciated what would become two simple
but powerful principles for the evolution of Canadian
cultural policy.

First, the means of distribution for cultural content should
be owned and controlled by Canadians.

Second, a corollary of the first, all foreign content in
Canada should be distributed by Canadians.

After Aird reported, an enormous struggle began over whether his recommendations should be implemented.

Quebec and some other provinces argued that the federal government did not have jurisdiction over the airwaves.

Skeptics in Canada did not believe that it was possible — or even, for certain interests, desirable — to resist the American media tide.

As the jurisdictional issue wound its way through the courts, two young men — Graham Spry and Alan Plaunt — created the Canadian Radio League to lobby for the creation of what would ultimately become the CBC.

Spry and Plaunt came from privileged backgrounds of wealth and influence. They were both clever. Spry had been a Rhodes scholar and met Plaunt while they were at Oxford. Together, they had been impressed by the British government's creation of the BBC. They resolved to accomplish something similar for Canada.

At the ages of twenty-six and thirty, with no staff or salaries, they went to work to forge a non-partisan coalition to press the government to follow Aird's recommendations. Animated by the same preoccupations about the influence of the Americans, Spry had argued that the choice was either "the State or the United States."

With their spectacular connections and heroic efforts, they managed to unite leaders from business, labour, religion, the universities and the newspapers to argue for the CBC. Almost all the presidents of the largest universities in the country came together, along with practically every editor and publisher of the most important newspapers. Spry and Plaunt's efforts have often been described as "the most successful lobbying campaign ever undertaken in Canada."

What is remarkable about Spry and Plaunt's achievement is the consensus that they established. It covered all parts of Canadian society and all stripes of political opinion. It was neither Liberal nor Conservative nor social democratic. It was — without becoming maudlin — simply Canadian.

The non-partisan coalition that the two men forged remained in place for decades. The extent of national agreement on cultural policy remained more or less intact well into the 1980s, when it began to fray under the pressures of the Canada–United States Free Trade Agreement and then — more profoundly — with the emergence of the FAANGs.

When federal jurisdiction was confirmed by the Judicial Committee of the Privy Council in London in 1932, the Conservative government of R.B. Bennett created the Canadian Radio Broadcasting Commission in the depths of the Depression.

Prime Minister Bennett reaffirmed Aird's conclusion that radio had to be Canadian-owned and -controlled. He said: "First of all, this country must be assured of the complete control of broadcasting from Canadian sources and free from foreign interference or influence. Without such control, broadcasting can never become a great agent for the diffusion of national thought and ideas . . ."[3]

This position was later strengthened by Mackenzie King's Liberals when they passed the *Broadcasting Act* of 1936, which formally changed the name of the Canadian Radio Broadcasting Commission to the Canadian Broadcasting Corporation.

Aird's report laid the basis for many of the policy innovations that were to be central to Canadian cultural life for the next four generations. In a moment of extraordinary prescience, he noted in 1932, at the age of almost eighty, that the government's work was far from over. "It is coming, gentlemen, and we should be prepared in dealing with this question of radio broadcasting to keep the question of television well before us."

In 1949, four years after the end of the Second World War, the Liberal government of Louis St. Laurent established the Royal Commission on National Development in the Arts, Letters and Sciences, led by Vincent Massey.

Like Aird twenty years earlier, Massey was preoccupied with the giant presence of the US just across the border. He wrote that: "American influences on Canadian life is to say the least impressive. There should be no thought of interfering with the liberty of all Canadians to enjoy them. Cultural exchanges are excellent in themselves . . . It cannot be denied, however, that a vast and disproportionate amount of material coming from a single alien source may stifle rather than stimulate our creative effort . . . We are now spending millions to maintain a national independence which would be nothing without a vigorous and distinctive cultural life."[4]

Massey went further and claimed that it was precisely the strength of Canada's culture — her "spiritual resources" — that helped it survive the Second World War. "Our country was sustained through difficult times by the power of this spiritual legacy. It will flourish in future in proportion as we believe in ourselves."[5]

The Massey Commission went on to make numerous recommendations, the most important of which proposed the creation of the Canada Council, the National Library and the Public Archives, as well as federal support for higher education and the strengthening of the National Film Board. But its most enduring contribution may be to have legitimized — once again — the importance of government action to offset the overwhelming influence of the US, so that we can "believe in ourselves."

When the Conservatives came into power in 1957, they had to consider what to do about the new medium of television. The CBC had begun broadcasting TV programs in 1952 and there was increasing pressure from the private radio broadcasters to allow them to do so as well.

In response, the government of John Diefenbaker followed the path laid out by Aird. It moved to license private television, but did so in a way that ensured all broadcasting in the country would contribute to the creation of a sense of national identity. It made clear that TV — like radio — "was to be essentially Canadian in content and character." It insisted that the first private TV stations in Canada be Canadian-owned and -controlled; and it created the first Canadian content quotas, requiring that private broadcasters fill more than half of their on-air hours with Canadian shows.

The new TV broadcasters could buy US shows (which were inexpensive and popular) and use them to attract Canadians. They could also be used to subsidize their more expensive Canadian ones.

This was the same strategy that had been pursued in radio. It followed Aird's second principle of using foreign content to support the creation of shows that were "Canadian in content and character."

But what did it mean to be "Canadian in content and character"? For the Conservatives of the early 1960s, it meant "any program made by a licensee, any production made in Canada, or a broadcast taking place outside Canada where Canadians are involved or have a special interest." Put more bluntly, in the early days of TV, a Canadian show was pretty much whatever the new stations made.

The question of what constitutes a Canadian show (or film or sound recording) has been a vexatious one. It lies at the very heart of Canadian cultural policy.

Historically, the definition has oscillated between two concepts. In the most common view, a show is Canadian if — as the Diefenbaker government specified — it is made by a Canadian company employing Canadians. This strangely industrial concept of Canadianness has been the standard for the last fifty-plus years.

Under current rules, a show is Canadian and qualifies for financial support if the company that produces it is owned and controlled by Canadians, and the key creative jobs (writer, lead actors, director, etc.) are Canadian. A production is scored on a 10-point system. The writer gets 2 points, the director 2 and the lead actors, composer, director of photography, editor and designer 1 point each. A show that scores 6/10 is eligible for tax credits; one that is 10/10 can receive tax credits and support from the Canada Media Fund (more on these later).

The problem with this approach is that it potentially allows programs that are shot and set in the US, with American characters and themes, to qualify as Canadian if they are made by Canadian companies with Canadian talent. Such shows would not, of course, be what Sir John Aird, Vincent Massey or the postwar Conservatives imagined when they set up the CBC or licensed private Canadian broadcasters. Such shows were precisely what they were trying to counter.

The alternative definition is that a show is Canadian if it is "culturally" Canadian. This means that the show is clearly set in Canada with Canadian characters, themes and stories. This approach has only been employed once, in the late nineties and only briefly then. It was used by the Canadian

Television Fund to ensure that the TV shows it financed were distinctly Canadian.

This is the third great issue that is central to Canadian cultural policy. Should government subsidies, whether tax credits, cash grants, money for the CBC or equity investments, help finance shows that are not clearly and identifiably Canadian? Or is it enough to say that whatever Canadians make, regardless of the stories explored or the setting of the program, should qualify for support?

In 1963, the Liberal government of Lester Pearson took power in Ottawa. The next half decade was a time of extraordinary ferment. In 1963, President Kennedy was assassinated. In 1968, Martin Luther King and Bobby Kennedy were killed; Paris experienced a near revolution in May; students throughout the Western world were occupying universities and demanding social change; everywhere, there were extensive demonstrations against the war in Vietnam.

The new Liberal government caught some of this spirit. It pursued an activist agenda that echoed the times. It reformed the social welfare system; opposed the war in Vietnam; welcomed a stream of American draft dodgers; and pursued policies that were avowedly nationalist in both economic and cultural policy.

At the heart of these changes was Judy LaMarsh, a broadcaster, lawyer and feminist. She was, as well, a charming, voluble and brilliant minister, who was only the second woman in the history of the country to sit in cabinet. She was responsible for much of the change initiated by the Pearson government, presiding over Canada's hundredth birthday and passing sweeping revisions to the *Broadcasting Act*. The revisions to the *Act* were once again non-partisan in the sense that they strengthened and solidified the policies that had been pursued by the Diefenbaker government and that had been pioneered by Sir John Aird.

The new *Act* reaffirmed and strengthened the garden's walls by requiring that all Canadian broadcasters, radio, TV and — for the first time — cable, had to be owned and controlled by Canadians. She reasoned that since "a distinctly Canadian broadcasting system is essential to our national identity, unity and vitality . . . in future, broadcasting may well be regarded as the central nervous system of Canadian nationhood . . . [so] it follows that the system must be effectively under Canadian ownership and control."[6]

The means of distribution had to be firmly and completely in Canadian hands. None of the foreign owners were grandfathered. They all had to sell their Canadian assets.

This resulted in a number of major American corporations being ordered to divest themselves of their Canadian cable and radio holdings.

The new *Act* created a wholly new regulator called the Canadian Radio Television Commission (CRTC). Its first chair was the formidable Pierre Juneau, a Jesuit-educated Canadian nationalist with a commanding presence and a fearless approach to his new job. He was, as well, a close colleague of the new prime minister, Pierre Trudeau, with whom he'd co-founded *Cité Libre*, the ferociously progressive counterblast to Duplessis' Age of Darkness.

One of Juneau's first tasks was to ensure that the ownership provisions of the *Act* were put into effect. This involved forcing a number of very large and well-connected US companies to sell their Canadian businesses.

Paramount and Famous Players were required to divest their jointly held cable TV company, Canadian Cable Corporation, which was a pioneer in the business and had been offering services since the late 1950s. They attempted to avoid complying, but, after much grumbling, sold it to Rogers Communications Inc. almost ten years later.

Similarly, RKO General, which had been one of the Big Five studios during Hollywood's golden age (and, beginning in 1955, a wholly owned subsidiary of General Tire and Rubber Company), was forced to divest its Windsor Station, CBLW. It was sold in a complex transaction engineered in part by Juneau to Baton Broadcasting and the CBC in 1970.

The puzzling thing about these forced divestitures was that there seemed to be little reaction by the American government. Typically — and certainly in future — the US would adamantly defend its companies' access to the Canadian market.

Later in life, when Juneau was president of the CBC, he was asked how much resistance there had been from the Americans. He replied: "Very little."

"Why do you think there was so little push back?" he was asked.

"I don't know. It was strange and very unlike the Americans. There was almost no complaint from the State Department or the embassy."

"Was it the brilliance of your management of the file?"

"No, no," he demurred. "Perhaps it was the Vietnam war. The Americans were feeling very beleaguered at the time. Maybe they just felt that they no longer had the moral capital to object."[7]

This never happened again. Over the next two decades, successive American governments, whether Democrat or Republican, would attack the Canadian government's cultural policies with extraordinary vigour. They used all the tools at their disposal to ensure that the garden was not extended beyond broadcasting. Both Jimmy Carter and Ronald Reagan used threats and legislation to try and overturn Sir John Aird's big principles.

The first skirmish came in 1972, when the CRTC moved to protect private Canadian broadcasters' business, which was based on buying Canadian rights to American shows to fill out their schedules and generate revenues.

The problem was that in some markets these rights were notional. All over Toronto — the biggest market in Canada — throughout the 1950s and '60s, people had put up antennae pointed at Buffalo so they could watch the big US networks: ABC, CBS and NBC. The same thing had happened in Vancouver, which was within range of stations in Blaine, Washington, that existed only to serve the Vancouver market.

The situation became worse with the emergence of cable. In the early days, the cable companies' key sales proposition was to deliver US signals to Canadian homes in high quality and without the vagaries associated with antennae. By expanding into areas beyond the reach of the US signals, they also made the US networks available almost everywhere in Canada.

Because the US border stations' signals could be received in Canada, they began selling advertising to Canadian businesses. In effect, they were competing with the private Canadian broadcasters and the CBC in their home markets.

To preserve the economic value of the rights that the Canadian broadcasters had bought, the CRTC began requiring the cable companies to strip the US ads from the signals of the border stations. This took a number of forms. At one point, the cable companies were ordered simply to delete the ads and replace them with public service announcements.

At another, they were ordered to delete the ads and replace them with the Canadian broadcasters' ads, a practice known as simultaneous substitution.

These policies were met with considerable hostility by the US border broadcasters and members of the US Congress. In July 1975, fourteen American senators wrote to the secretary of state, Henry Kissinger, demanding that he "take a more active role in protecting the legitimate interests of those stations."[8]

Pierre Juneau met his American counterpart, Richard Wiley, the head of the Federal Communications Commission to discuss the issue. The meetings were described as ". . . heated, with neither official giving an inch."[9]

Furious with the Canadian position, the border broadcasters described commercial deletion as ". . . something approaching theft and piracy" and the only response to this would be jamming their signals, denying Canadians access to them, a measure which they "would reluctantly — genuinely more in sorrow than anger — adopt."[10]

For their part, Canadian officials like Communications Minister Gérard Pelletier — another member of the *Cité Libre* set — made fun of the American concerns, saying that jamming the signals would be absurd. In a long article entitled "Pelletier Ridicules U.S. Threat to Jam TV signals in Ontario," the *Globe and Mail* outlined all the reasons why the government found the border broadcasters' position idiotic.[11]

At the same time, the *New York Times* attacked the government, calling the commercial deletion policy "shabby, sleazy, shady, morally dishonest, beneath contempt."[12]

While this controversy raged on, the government introduced new legislation that would further aggravate relations between the two countries. To reinforce the walls of the garden, the government passed Bill C-58, which disallowed advertising as a legitimate business expense when purchased on foreign media. The bill was designed to make it uneconomical for Canadian companies to advertise on the US border stations.

It was also aimed at ensuring that the magazine industry was firmly in Canadian hands. Of particular concern was the practice of both *Time* and *Reader's Digest* of producing "split-run" editions, which were printed in Canada and had Canadian ads, but were identical to the US editions in content. The Canadian magazines complained that this practice was unfair, since neither *Time* nor *Reader's Digest* had to bear the costs of producing original Canadian content.

The government ruled that for *Time* and *Reader's Digest* to qualify as Canadian for tax treatment, they would have to create Canadian editions that were 75 per cent Canadian-owned and not "substantially the same" as their US editions. Not "substantially the same" was defined as having 80 per cent different content from the US edition. Ultimately, *Reader's Digest* found a way to conform to the new rules, but *Time* did not.

C-58 was, in effect, a way of extending the garden policy to magazines and ensuring that Canadian advertising revenue stayed with Canadian media as much as possible. It also reinforced the garden for newspapers, since the papers would always be more valuable to Canadian owners than to foreigners.

None of this was well-received in the United States. American politicians fulminated against the new rules, egged on by *Time* and the border broadcasters. In retribution, the

US Congress passed its own tax law barring write-offs for any association that held a conference in Canada.

The controversy became so heated that it almost resulted in a breakdown in relations between the two governments. In 1975, the departing US ambassador, William J. Porter, briefed Canadian journalists on US unhappiness with the increasingly nationalist stance of the Trudeau government. He mentioned particularly C-58 and the fact that *Time* and *Reader's Digest* had threatened to close their Canadian editions.[13]

The US ambassador's public rebuke of the government's policies enraged the cabinet so much that the prime minister and other senior ministers refused to attend his farewell party. Trudeau called US President Gerald Ford to complain. So testy did things become that the foreign ministers — Henry Kissinger and Allan MacEachen — took time out from meetings in Paris to put out a statement reaffirming the close and cordial relationship between the two countries.

Over the years, the US government continued the pressure, demanding changes to the legislation. The matter would blow up on a fairly regular basis, with the US citing C-58 as an ongoing irritant. Both Liberal and Conservative governments, however, held firm, maintaining the bipartisan consensus on the importance of the garden policy. They did so even when the stakes were very high and the pressure to accede tremendous.

The Liberals not only maintained the garden strategy, they also started to water the plants. In 1983, Communications Minister Francis Fox set up the Canadian Broadcast Development Fund — the first system, apart from financing for the CBC, that directly subsidized the production of Canadian TV shows. Fox provided Telefilm, which had previously only been involved with movies, resources to help finance programs made by independent producers for the major Canadian networks. This laid the groundwork for the creation of the vast array of support measures — the tax credits and the Canada Media Fund — that would be put in place over the next thirty years to assist the creation of Canadian drama, comedy, documentaries and children's programs.

The Americans did not object.

As we shall see, the Americans never object to the government providing direct subsidies to the production of Canadian cultural products. Why should they? Subsidies do not take anything away from American broadcasters; and if the result is to produce a book or film that might draw an international audience, then the American publisher or film distributor will simply outbid their Canadian counterparts for it.

As the Liberal regime came to an end, the US interests saw their moment. Thomas Wyman, the chairman of CBS, led a study on the problems with Canadian cultural policy. It was not conceived as a dispassionate analysis of the issues. He simply phoned his friends and asked what was bothering them.

The report was issued in September 1984. *Trade Barriers to U.S. Motion Pictures and TV, Pre-recorded Entertainment, Publishing and Advertising Industries* was basically a list of gripes that annoyed the Americans and was intended as a checklist for the US government to resolve. It arrived as a welcome card for the new Conservative government.

CHAPTER 3

Expanding the Garden: The Mulroney Years

In 1984, Brian Mulroney and the Conservatives danced into power. Campaigning on a market-friendly platform, they won the greatest mandate in Canadian history. During the campaign, they had emphasized the need to reverse many of the previous government's economic policies. Where the Liberals had been nationalist, the Tories promoted foreign investment; where the Liberals had been interventionist, the Tories favoured free markets; where the Liberals had fought incessantly with the Americans, the Tories wanted to repair relations. Their policies were — on their face — completely incompatible with many of the cultural initiatives that had been taken by their predecessors.

The most visible and symbolically charged moment for the new government occurred at the Shamrock Summit in March 1985, when President Reagan and his wife came to Quebec City. It culminated in the prime minister, the president and their wives singing "When Irish Eyes Are Smiling."

During the course of the summit, the US and Canadian sides discussed the possibility of negotiating more open trade arrangements between the two countries. A few

months afterward, Mulroney announced that the government wanted to see whether it was possible to negotiate a
free trade agreement with the Americans.

This was a very daring and controversial undertaking.
Free trade with the US had always been the worst and ugli-
est bogeyman for English Canadian nationalists. They feared
that the tide of American culture would become overwhelming; they feared, as well, that the garden strategy would have
to be abandoned, resulting in — as the Massey Commission
put it — Canada being intellectually and spiritually annexed
to the US.

When Mulroney put together his first cabinet in late 1984,
he named as minister of communications — effectively the
minister of culture — Marcel Masse, a conservative Quebec
nationalist of the old Union Nationale party that had run
Quebec for much of the postwar period. His appointment
was not surprising in the sense that the Conservatives had
won their huge majority by reaching out to the soft nationalists in Quebec; it was surprising, however, in the sense that
the Union Nationale had always been — as the very name
suggested — strongly committed to maintaining traditional
Quebec culture.

Whether the prime minister understood at the time that
Masse wanted to extend the Union Nationale's policies
to Canadian culture as a whole — pulling in the opposite
direction of the government's overall stance — is not clear.
Whether that was something that Mulroney wanted as a
counterweight to his deregulatory and free trade agenda
is also not clear. But whatever Mulroney had in mind, the
appointment of Masse laid the basis for a tremendous debate
about the centrality of cultural nationalism to Canadian
public life.

Masse was a compelling figure. He was vain, clever, charming when he wanted to be, passionate, handsome, voluble, hard-working and arrogant. The English Canadian cultural nationalists fell in love with him almost immediately. His cabinet colleagues took a dimmer view, regarding him as a nuisance at best and at worst a one-man wrecking crew for the government's overall agenda.

From the moment Masse started as minister of communications, it became clear that he would be a minister unlike all others.

At the time, I was the director general of strategy in the department, working for the deputy minister, Robert Rabinovitch. It had been my job to prepare the briefing books for the new minister and organize the first round of meetings between him and the officials in the department. At the time, there were only three of these who really mattered: the deputy minister; the senior assistant deputy minister, Alain Gourd; and the assistant deputy minister for cultural policy, David Silcox.

From the beginning, Masse made a number of things very clear. First, he wanted to work only in French. He wanted every memo, every cabinet document, every conversation and every briefing to be in French. As he noted, sensibly enough, "You would not ask an English Cabinet minister to work in French. Why ask a French minister to work in English?" This would prove to be a challenge.

It also became clear that he was a cultural enthusiast. Not all culture ministers are. Most pretend an interest, but often know very little and care less. Not Masse. He loved all aspects of culture: museums, art galleries, music festivals, books, movies, dance, theatre. He also believed that the arts were the key to the identity of a country; and without a clear and strong sense of identity, there was no point having a country at all.

In a quote that introduced his grand theory of cultural sovereignty to the Canadian cabinet in late 1985, he cited Albert Camus: "Without a culture and the relative freedom it presumes, society even when perfect, is a jungle."

Many of his colleagues in the cabinet did not share his views; many found them pretentious and patronizing.

It became clear, as well, that he thought the public service was infected with Liberals. His particular ire fell upon the deputy minister, Robert Rabinovitch, who, along with another senior official, Ed Clark, were regarded by the Conservatives as being responsible for the much-reviled National Energy Program that had outraged Alberta and helped the Tories win the election. Rabinovitch and Clark were marked by the new administration as die-hard Liberals, probably socialists, who had to be watched and — if possible — dismissed.

Ultimately they were both fired. If they were socialists, their subsequent careers were peculiar. Rabinovitch, with a Ph.D. from Wharton in finance, became chief operating officer at Claridge, the Bronfman family's investment bank; Clark, with a Ph.D. in economics from Harvard, became CEO of the Toronto-Dominion Bank.

In the fall of 1984, however, Masse assumed that Rabinovitch was bending his energies to the undoing of the new Conservative government. At one point, he asked me, "Do you know why the red maple leaf is on the flag?"

"No," I said.

"Because it is the colour of the Liberals. It's designed to make Canadians think that the Liberals are the country."

"That seems a little far-fetched," I offered.

"You are naïve, Richard," he continued. "Nothing with the Liberals is an accident."

Masse's sense that he was dealing with a potentially treacherous deputy fed his paranoia. This was reinforced by his office. His most influential advisor, Patricia Finlay — his conduit to the most rabid members of the Canadian nationalist community in Toronto — shared his views about Liberals under the bed.

Masse's passion for culture and his paranoia were potentiated by his intelligence, his charm and his hyperactive work ethic. He was full of ideas. All the time. Day and night. He would call at all hours, suggesting new initiatives and arguments. Sometimes he thought up a new museum that the country had to have (a comedy museum, a humour museum, a photography museum), sometimes a new piece of research that needed to be done, sometimes just a nugget of useful gossip. He loved gossip. The staff meetings would always begin with the question: *"Quels sont les rumeurs, Richard?"*

It was not clear that he slept very much. He was constantly reading, travelling, talking (endlessly talking), visiting arts organizations or boning up on the details of his portfolio. We made a set of flash cards for him with a question about Canadian culture on one side and the answer on the other. What percentage of the box office in Canada goes to domestic films? Three per cent. What percentage of Canadian films are produced or distributed by the major American studios? Zero per cent. He would use his detailed grasp of the facts to wow his audiences and intimidate his colleagues.

So busy and full of ideas was he that I had to develop a way of protecting the rest of the department from his enthusiasms, lest it drown. The problem was that he would often have an idea one day, only to forget it the next. There was, of course, no point in doing a lot of work on something that was not going anywhere and was but a moment's infatuation.

The form protection took was the Three-Request Rule. If Masse asked for a piece of work to be done, I would say that we would get right on it and do nothing. If he mentioned it a second time, I would say that we were studying the matter and do nothing. Only when he asked a third time, when it was clear that it mattered to him, would I ask people in the department to initiate the necessary work.

I never told him about the Three-Request Rule until he was out of office.

"You see," he said. "I was right to be suspicious."

Masse also came to his responsibilities with a coherent view of how cultural policy should be pursued. It is rare for new culture ministers to have any ideas at all, save perhaps for a vague enthusiasm for the arts. It is completely unheard of for a minister to arrive in the portfolio with a sophisticated view of what needed to be done.

Masse believed that the solution to Canada's chronic cultural weakness was to extend the garden beyond radio and TV to books, sound recording and film. He wanted to place the means of distribution in Canadian hands and force the foreign — almost always American — product through those channels. This would, he believed, strengthen the Canadian companies financially, so that they could produce more and better Canadian content.

Masse's view of the garden was supplemented by his belief that only Canadians would or could produce Canadian books, music and movies. Foreigners, he reasoned, had no interest in making Canadian films or shows. Why would they? They were not Canadian; Canada did not matter to them.

The facts bore him out. Canadian films were over-whelmingly produced by Canadian producers, Canadian records by Canadian labels, Canadian books by Canadian publishers. The facts were clear and had been for a long time.

His view of what to do was also intensely conservative. He did not like the idea of giving grants and subsidies to film makers, writers and musicians. He preferred a system where the companies that employed them were financially successful enough to pay them properly. Grants smacked of elite charity; it was better for a real market to finance cultural products.

Besides, after the government hands out the subsidy, what then? How will the film makers' movies get to a screen, the writers' books to a bookstore, the musicians' work to their listeners? If they are made but not distributed, what is the point? If a tree falls in the forest . . .

Masse came to call his version of the garden strategy cultural sovereignty. The phrase captured the Quebec nationalist impulse (*maîtres chez nous*). It was, as well, consistent with the approach that successive Canadian governments — both Liberal and Conservative — had taken to the problem.

The difficulty for Masse was that the concept of cultural sovereignty appeared to be at odds with the new govern-ment's desire to repair relations with the US. It not only reminded everyone of the vexatious policies the Trudeau government had pursued with C-58, simultaneous substitu-tion and the forced divestiture of American broadcasting assets, it made clear that it wanted to extend them into other areas that were extremely valuable and important to very powerful US companies.

At the same time, the new government said that it not only wanted to improve relations with the US, but wanted actively to embrace it by entering into a free trade agreement. It was hard for most ministers and most Canadians to see how restricting entry in the cultural area could be squared with encouraging it everywhere else. It was difficult to imagine a less propitious moment to launch a major new set of policies to strengthen Canada's cultural sovereignty.

To pursue his agenda, Masse would need the senior officials in the department to be on side. His problem was that he thought that they would not help, either because they were closet Liberals or because their career loyalties would be with the government's overall agenda and not his. This was particularly true of the two officials who would be most central to his ambitions: the deputy, Robert Rabinovitch and the assistant deputy, David Silcox.

David Silcox was immensely knowledgeable. He had been one of the founders of the Canada Council's book program, was Canada's leading authority on both the Group of Seven and David Milne and was brilliantly connected in the English cultural community. He had also been a canoeing pal of Pierre Trudeau, doubtless a black mark for Masse.

Masse's worst suspicions were confirmed when, rather than simply backing his ideas unquestioningly, Rabinovitch and Silcox pushed back. They would explain the limits of what could be done, the other options he might consider and how his proposals would be received in the rest of the government. He took this as disloyalty, rather than an opportunity to craft what he wanted in a way that would be broadly acceptable.

For Masse, then, and his office, an essential step in advancing their policy objectives was to drive out Rabinovitch. They succeeded, but received a new deputy whose loyalties were equally doubtful. De Montigny Marchand, like Rabinovitch, had had an excellent education and a distinguished career in the public service. He had been trained as a lawyer and honoured as a Queen's Counsel. He was, as well, extremely knowledgeable both about the department and the government as a whole, having been assistant deputy minister for policy at the department and, after that, deputy secretary to the cabinet.

He was named deputy minister in part to get Marcel Masse under control and better aligned with the government's overall priorities. He was sly and clever. And equally importantly, he was fully conversant with the Quebec cultural references that animated Masse's thoughts and ideas. He was more than a match for the determined and ambitious minister.

Unfortunately, like Rabinovitch, Marchand thought it was his job to give the minister independent advice. This further soured relationships among the minister, his office and the department. Things went from bad to worse. The department was accused of not responding to the minister's instructions; the minister and his office were accused of arrogance, willful misunderstanding and incompetence. The whole situation became very tense.

Not getting the responses they wanted from the department, the minister's office staff began to draft policy itself. They started with a new book-publishing policy. It was the brainchild of Patricia Finlay, aided by Paul Audley, a cultural policy consultant from Toronto with a strong nationalist bent. He had done extensive work on the publishing business in Canada for what would become the Association of Canadian Publishers.

Audley was an expert on the facts of the business: Seventy-five per cent of all the books in Canadian bookstores were American and came from American publishers, who also had an iron grip on the textbook market in Canada, the most lucrative part of the business. Their Canadian business made up half their foreign sales, twice as much as they sold in the UK.

For their part, the Canadian publishers were very small and undercapitalized. Most of them lived on knife edges of imminent insolvency. Despite their feeble circumstances, they were overwhelmingly the most important publishers of Canadian books.

The Canadian publishers had complained for many years that the foreigners enjoyed advantages unavailable to their Canadian counterparts. In particular, they had the benefits of vastly larger home markets that allowed them to lay off their costs across a much bigger base. This, in turn, allowed them to "dump" their product in Canada at prices and terms the Canadians could not match. As a result, they dominated all the most lucrative parts of the book market.

The Canadian publishers had warned that — as with radio and TV — letting foreigners overwhelm the market for books in Canada was culturally dangerous and incompatible with building a distinct country in the northern half of the continent.

They argued that if the foreign books coming into Canada were distributed by Canadian publishers themselves, they would be able to make more money, which they would then use to produce and distribute more Canadian books. They suggested, in effect, that the government pursue a publishing version of the garden strategy that Sir John Aird had championed fifty years earlier.

The proposal that Masse's office put together — and that he took to cabinet — was much weaker than the 1968 *Broadcasting Act*. It did not suggest that all the foreign publishers in Canada be forced to sell their businesses to Canadians. Rather, it proposed that limits be placed on their ability to buy Canadian publishing houses and that, when a foreign publisher operating in Canada was sold as part of a larger transaction outside the country, the new owner be obliged to sell the Canadian branch to Canadians. This latter — and ultimately highly controversial — requirement was referred to as an "indirect" acquisition. It was called "indirect" to make it sound as though the acquisition of the Canadian subsidiary of the foreign publisher was not central to whatever the transaction happened to be, and, therefore, of little consequence.

The most famous example occurred when Gulf and Western, a large US entertainment conglomerate, bought the giant textbook publisher Prentice Hall. When it did, it also acquired Prentice Hall's publishing business in Canada. Under the terms of the new policy, Gulf and Western would be obliged to sell the Canadian part of Prentice Hall's business in Canada to Canadians.

The policy was not wrong-headed. It was conceptually consistent with past practice. The problem was that it had not been carefully thought through, and the way it was designed would ultimately prove to be catastrophic. With good intentions, but limited experience, Masse's office produced a policy that would poison the well for years to come.

While the minister's office was merrily working away, David Silcox announced that he had had enough and that he was resigning. It was a shame. If he had been properly consulted and trusted, he might have made the new publishing policy into a workable plan. But he was not. Later, like Rabinovitch and Ed Clark, he would enjoy significant career success, becoming deputy minister of culture in Ontario and president of Sotheby's Canada.

To replace him, de Montigny Marchand organized a competition for his job. I applied. Why? I do not know. Blind ambition perhaps. Simple foolishness? Whatever the motivation, I did not get the job.

The candidate that Marchand wanted was Jeremy Kinsman, the head of political affairs at the embassy in Washington. He was an almost perfect choice. Well-educated at Princeton and Science Po (originally the École Nationale des Sciences Politiques), fluently bilingual and knowledgeable about how to deal with Americans. Kinsman was, in fact, the superior candidate and was declared the winner by the Public Service Commission.

Masse was enraged. He did not want Kinsman. The embassy in Washington was then seen as one of the biggest impediments to the new publishing policy. The ambassador, Allan Gotlieb, had savaged it on a number of occasions. Masse feared that Kinsman would be a stooge for the mandarins at foreign affairs, who wanted nothing to do with cultural sovereignty. It was also rumoured that Masse's advisor, Patricia Finlay, did not want Kinsman, feeling that he would not be sufficiently loyal. As Kinsman himself later observed, joining the department in those days was like joining the mob: you had to kill your sister to demonstrate your trustworthiness.

Marchand pushed back, but he could not advance Kinsman's nomination. The process stalled. At this point, Masse began manoeuvring to get rid of Marchand, who was seen, like Rabinovitch, as disloyal, someone who would not obediently do the minister's bidding.

Masse took his new policy to cabinet in the spring of 1985. It was not well received. Concerns were expressed about it being half-baked. Ministers questioned how it would be implemented. What if no Canadian publisher wanted to buy the asset that had to be divested as the result of an "indirect" takeover? What if the price asked was too high? What if the Canadians could not raise enough money?

More importantly, concerns were expressed that the policy would anger the Americans and compromise the government's ability to get a free trade deal. Masse replied by arguing that taking a strong stand on culture would make a deal easier to sell to Canadians. They would be reassured that they would be able to continue to be themselves and not be turned into little Americans.

Ultimately, despite its reservations, the cabinet agreed during a retreat in Mulroney's home town of Baie-Comeau, Quebec. Masse immediately left the meeting room and rushed to the waiting microphones to announce Canada's new book policy, which became known as the Baie-Comeau policy. Masse confided later that he felt he had to announce it immediately or the dark forces of finance and foreign affairs would find a way to undo the cabinet's decision.

After the announcement, I was asked to organize a retreat for the minister, his office and the senior departmental officials to overcome the problems between us. The idea was to spend a couple of days together at the Château Montebello to see if the relationship could be put on a better footing. I dutifully drew up a set of briefing books and drafted an agenda designed to help us resolve our differences.

The retreat fell apart from the very beginning. Masse kicked it off by launching into a very detailed denunciation of the department and its inadequacies. He went on for what seemed like an eternity. The senior officials looked stricken; the members of his office looked triumphant. "All right," Masse said at the end of his diatribe, "Let's move on to the agenda."

"Whoa," Marchand said. "Just before we discuss anything else, I have a few bones to pick myself." He then launched into a ferocious denunciation of Masse, his office and the various calumnies they had perpetrated. He did not mention the dispute over Kinsman's candidacy for assistant deputy minister, but his rebuttal was personal, angry and direct.

At the end of his speech, a great silence fell across the meeting room. It was clear that we were at a terrible impasse. There was no longer any common ground at all. There was only ruin and scorched earth as far as the eye could see. The attempt to improve relations had failed utterly. Everyone looked at each other in shocked silence.

The rest of the day is a blur. There were listless discussions of items on the agenda, but no conclusions. There were also rumours circulating. Marchand looked too relaxed after shredding the minister. The minister also looked too relaxed, although he kept out of sight most of the time, sitting in his room, smoking his small black cigars and plotting.

Later in the afternoon, there was an announcement in Ottawa. Marchand was out. Alain Gourd was in. Masse was now on to his third deputy minister in less than a year. It was not clear who had won, Marchand or Masse.

Gourd arrived to much fanfare. He had been in Ottawa, trying to sort out the first of the innumerable problems of Baie-Comeau. He was thirty-eight years old, very young for a deputy. We all knew him well, but his ascension cast him in a new light. We hoped that he would be able to work more effectively with the minister than Rabinovitch or Marchand.

Certainly, he seemed potentially better-suited. He had studied law and philosophy and worked in his family's radio business before coming to Ottawa. He was sunny, with a subtle and flexible caste of mind. His manner was always gracious, if a little studied and formal. I could easily tell when he was displeased with me. Instead of simply addressing me by my name, he would call me "*cher* Richard"; when he was very annoyed, I became "*mon cher* Richard." I thought he had the right temperament to deal with Masse and his office.

He set immediately to work, reorganizing the department and repopulating its upper ranks. He promoted me to assistant deputy minister, but not to replace David Silcox. I asked him why not. He said he had to prove to the mandarins in Ottawa that he was not Masse's poodle; therefore the job had to go to Kinsman.

Whether that was true was hard to say. The Public Service Commission forced Gourd to begin a new process to fill the job, which he did. Kinsman applied again and won again. Somehow Gourd managed to get Masse to accept his appointment and he joined the department in the late fall of 1985, inheriting the problematic Baie-Comeau policy.

The finale of the day took place after dinner. Masse made a little speech, Gourd made a little speech, I made a little speech and David Silcox said farewell. He appeared before everyone wearing a baseball hat with the letters KMAGYOYO on it. He began by addressing Masse: "You have always accused me of being a Liberal. Well, given what I have seen, I probably am. So I wore this hat tonight to summarize my feelings about our time together. It is basically an old army saying from the Second World War. The letters stand for: Kiss My Ass Goodbye. You're On Your Own."

And with that, Silcox smiled, waved and left the room and the department.

The first test of the Baie-Comeau policy arose with Gulf and Western's acquisition of Prentice Hall. Although the transaction had taken place before the policy was announced, an effort was made to apply it retroactively. Not surprisingly, Gulf and Western objected, as did many parts of the Canadian government. Allan Gotlieb, the Canadian ambassador to the US, wrote to the minister in charge, saying that the publishing policy was "ill timed, unclear and likely to damage the progress Ottawa had made recapturing the affection of American investors . . . Gulf and Western would adopt a 'scorched earth response' if its acquisition of Prentice Hall was blocked."

As it turned out, the government caved and the Prentice Hall acquisition was approved, along with the purchase of a small Canadian textbook branch plant, Ginn Canada. The latter takeover was subject to a requirement that 51 per cent of Ginn be sold to Canadians within two years.[1]

During that period, the landscape changed: the Canada–United States Free Trade Agreement came into effect. Among its final arrangements was a requirement that the government of Canada buy 51 per cent of any company divested under Baie-Comeau at a "fair open market value."[2] Gulf and Western probably reasoned that the government of Canada had deeper pockets than the chronically impoverished Canadian publishers and would pay a higher price, which is precisely what happened.

In May 1989, the Canada Development Investment Corporation bought 51 per cent of Ginn and a smaller company (named GLC) for $10.3 million. But Gulf and Western, now owned by Paramount, kept five of the eight board seats and had a veto over "significant operating decisions." The result was that the foreign assets did not end up in the hands of Canadian publishers, but rather in the hands of the government, while the foreigners still maintained control. It was difficult not to conclude that Baie-Comeau's first major test case had turned the policy into something of a fiasco.

Following the Ginn and GLC debacle, a number of other transactions were subject to the Baie-Comeau policy, with wildly inconsistent results. Some foreign publishers were allowed to buy Canadian companies. Longman Pearson was allowed to purchase Copp Clark and Penguin bought New American Library. In other cases, the policy was circumvented by delaying tactics on the part of the acquirers. Robert Maxwell managed to hold on to Collier Macmillan Canada for almost six years before Investment Canada came to a ruling. Still others, like Harcourt Brace Jovanovich, evaded the policy by selling 51 per cent to Canadians, but keeping all the voting shares and control.

After its first seven years in existence, the Baie-Comeau policy was a mess. Of more than a dozen cases of foreign takeovers of publishing assets in Canada, only five were successfully patriated. And of those five, some were patriated in name only, with control remaining in the hands of foreigners.

Eventually, the Conservatives threw in the towel. In 1992, Perrin Beatty, then the minister of communications, replaced Baie-Comeau with a "net benefits test." This meant that foreign takeovers of Canadian publishers would not be blocked or require divestiture of control, but would be allowed if the acquirers could show that the takeovers were of "benefit" to Canada. This change effectively gutted the policy.

The final undoing of the policy occurred under the new Liberal government of Jean Chrétien. In 1994, five years after the Canadian government bought Ginn and GLC, it sold them back to the original owners for the same price that it had paid in 1989. The first and most important test case was unwound and the policy was buried.

The failure of Baie-Comeau was attributable in part to the political climate of the times. The fact that the government was trying to negotiate the free trade agreement gave the Americans enormous leverage. They could threaten to end the talks if they did not receive concessions. When the government had to choose between books and the rest of the economy, it really had no choice.

More importantly, however, the policy was wrong-headed in a number of ways. It was, from the outset, poorly conceived and badly implemented. Unlike the Canadianization of the broadcasting system, there was no clear set of rules that would apply to everyone transparently and uniformly. Rather, decisions were made on a case-by-case basis without any consistency. Inevitably, this made the policy into a muddle and led to charges — correctly — that it was arbitrary.

The failure of Baie-Comeau rippled out beyond books. The government's inability to extend the garden to publishing would have implications for future efforts to do so for feature films. In both cases — movies and books — the failure to place the means of distribution in Canadian hands would ultimately mean that these industries struggled and that Canadian culture suffered accordingly.

As we've seen, it was relatively early in the life of the Mulroney government that it set its sights on negotiating a free trade agreement with the US. Not just the Baie-Comeau policy but cultural policy overall was a sticking point.

The key question was how the cultural industries were to be treated in the trade deal. The Americans took the view that TV shows, books and films were simply "entertainment" and did not deserve any special status. They should be treated the same as hogs or aluminium.

As Samuel Goldwyn once observed: "Nobody ever called it show art; it's show business." For the United States, the cultural industries were also very big businesses. In the 1980s, American "entertainment" generated a "trade surplus . . . second only to the defence industry."[3]

But even more importantly, the export of US films and TV shows helped define what was "cool" in markets all over the world — namely, the cars, clothes, food, music and lifestyle choices shown on screen. American films and TV shows were a giant, enormously effective marketing tool for everything else that the United States had to sell.

The US negotiators were perfectly aware of how important the entertainment industries were for US trade. They insisted from the outset of the talks that culture was on the table. The most senior American officials made clear that they wanted not only to preserve the access to the Canadian market they already had, they also wanted to target the policies they actively disliked, including "those affecting U.S. border stations, foreign investment rules forcing the sale of book publishing firms to Canadian investors" and everything else they had fought and lost over the years.

This was wildly controversial in cultural nationalist circles. It was seen as potentially an existential threat to the very notion of an independent Canada.

Leading Canadians warned of its potential dangers. All across the political spectrum, media people, artists, intellectuals, publishers, film makers, editorialists and opposition politicians sounded the same alarm. They insisted that whatever the trade talks were about, they could not be about culture. They could not involve dismantling the garden; they could not involve pulling down the subsidies for books and films and TV. Culture had to be off the table.

The Americans did not help the situation. They insisted that culture had to be *on* the table. They ridiculed the Canadians' preoccupations as simply a blind to protect their "entertainment" industries from competition. They failed to see what all the fuss was about. They buttressed their position by pointing to all the bad things that the Canadians had done. They pointed to commercial deletion, C-58 and the Baie-Comeau policy.

The Mulroney government itself was split. Parts of it wanted to see culture exempted from the trade talks, while other parts feared that asking for an exemption might ruin the chance of getting a deal at all.

As the government was preparing to begin negotiations on the free trade agreement, Masse decided to push on beyond books and publishing. With Alain Gourd as his new deputy and Jeremy Kinsman freshly installed as the head of cultural policy, he decided to bring to cabinet a complete theory of cultural sovereignty.

The entire resources of the department were drawn into the creation of his masterwork. Everyone toiled like mad dogs, working nights, weekends and holidays to produce the definitive, all-singing, all-dancing version of the doctrine of cultural sovereignty. When it was finally finished, it was almost 280 pages long, describing in detail what needed to be done. It was also only available in French.

The text itself made the case that culture was central to the life of the country and that it ought to be accorded the same priority as national security. Without a distinct culture, there was no country and nothing to defend.

It argued that only Canadians will make Canadian culture. Canadian ownership of the key means of cultural production and distribution was, therefore, fundamental and needed to be extended to sound recording and film, as had already been done for books, magazines and TV.

The document recognized that many of Canada's cultural companies were woefully undercapitalized and would not be able to afford the acquisition of foreign assets that would give effect to the policy. It proposed to create a cultural bank to resolve this problem.

Finally, it argued strenuously that culture had to be exempted from the free trade agreement. This was essential not just to safeguard Canada's sovereignty, but also to reassure Canadians that they would be able to retain their identity when the free trade agreement was concluded. Without an exemption, it would be very difficult to sell the deal to the public.

The vast document included helpful statistics, hortatory quotes from important artists and intellectuals and a series of annexes, explaining how the different policies that it proposed would work. It was a formidably dense piece of work, a veritable "brick."

When the draft paper on cultural sovereignty was circulated for comment, the reaction was uniformly hostile. Officials from finance, foreign affairs, the Privy Council Office and the Treasury Board all came to the meetings to denounce our efforts.

They complained that the brick was too long; we explained that French texts were always longer than English ones. They complained that it was only in French; we pointed out that French was an official language. They complained that the evidence was poor; we argued it was incontrovertible. They said it would sink the free trade talks; we countered that the free trade agreement could not be sold without it.

And so it went. Back and forth. A dialogue of the deaf.

As the brick was winding its way through the consultation process, occasional smoke signals would emerge from important quarters, suggesting that despite the gripes of officials, we were on the right course.

In a speech in Chicago around this time, the prime minister said, "When it comes to discussing better trade rules for our cultural industries, you will have to understand that what we call cultural sovereignty is as vital to our national life as political sovereignty." It appeared that there was support at the top. Heartened, we carried on.

The brick was taken up by cabinet in early 1986. It was even more poorly received than the Baie-Comeau policy. Many ministers were furious. In a particularly angry outburst, Michael Wilson, the finance minister, accused Masse of "sabotaging" the free trade talks.[4] The brick was effectively stonewalled. Its contents were never released.

Within Ottawa, serious discussions had begun about how to deal with Masse. Gourd, Kinsman and I were called to a lunch with two of the most senior officials in the capital. They were there to read us the riot act. They were also there to make clear that our careers were in peril.

"Your Minister is out of control," they began. "You are failing in your duties. He is making everyone crazy."

"What would you like us to do?" Gourd asked.

"Get him under control," they replied.

"Have you met M. Masse?" Gourd asked.

"No."

"Then you have no idea what you are asking."

"Whether we have met him or not is irrelevant. It's your job to get him under control."

We did not want to be unhelpful, because these were genuinely important people. But it was hard to square the circle. When Rabinovitch and Marchand had tried to rein Masse in, they had been sacked or transferred. Besides, did we not have a duty to help Masse pursue his agenda as best we could? After all, the prime minister had given him the job.

The lunch went on for about an hour with no real resolution. We felt like we were being assigned an impossible task. It was disheartening and frightening to be attacked by such senior people.

"I guess we are in shit," I said to Kinsman. "They don't seem to like us."

"It's bad, all right," he replied. "But I think they understand that we are good guys with bad files."

"More like toxic files," I replied.

"Yeah, good guys with toxic files."

I was not so sure we could leave it like that. I had small children and a mortgage to pay. For that matter, so did Kinsman. The lunch worried me; I did not want to lose my job or be sidelined to a nothing position in the department of small animal husbandry.

With the failure at cabinet, the mood in the communications department darkened. It darkened, as well, in the nationalist community, as word of Masse's defeat trickled out. In a powerful letter to the editor of the *Globe and Mail*, Margaret Atwood captured the fear that many felt. "Canadian people, like people everywhere, have values other than money that are important to them. Their fears of losing these values are real fears . . . It's no use claiming that there is some mysterious gene of Canadianness welded into us at conception that will guarantee the retention of these values if all the social structures and . . . cultural manifestations of them disappear."[5]

There was much discussion about how to respond. At one of our meetings, Masse suggested that I do something or another in a couple of weeks' time. With some relief, I told him that I had to be in Paris then for meetings. I was looking forward to getting out of town and the increasingly oppressive circumstances of being "a good guy with toxic files."

"Paris," he said. "Excellent. The Musée des Beaux Arts in Montreal is having an exhibition of Leonardo the engineer. Why don't you borrow the *Mona Lisa* while you are there. It would make a great addition to the show."

"The *Mona Lisa*?"

This was the part of Masse that I liked: the vaulting and sometimes preposterous ambition. I went away to study the matter. When I next discussed it with him, I explained that the *Mona Lisa* had only been loaned twice since the Second World War.

"The first time," I said, "was in the early 1960s. The Kennedys were having dinner with André Malraux, the French minister of culture. Jackie asked to borrow the picture."

"Ah, Malraux," he said. "And what did he say to Jackie?"

"He said 'Yes.'"

"Excellent. And the second time?"

"The second, they loaned it to the Japanese in exchange for landing rights for the Concorde. What shall I say we will offer them?"

"Why, my best wishes, of course."

"That's it?"

"It was good enough for Malraux. But you can add that I will be much obliged."

What does one do with that? I had not the heart to remind him that he was neither Jackie Kennedy nor landing rights in Tokyo.

I went to Paris and shortly after, in May 1986, the government began formal negotiations with the Americans on the free trade agreement. To clear the decks and limit barracking from the peanut gallery, the prime minister shuffled Masse off to the Department of Energy in June.

He was replaced by Flora MacDonald.

She was, in many ways, the opposite of Masse. Where he was arrogant and aloof, she was down-to-earth. Where he was cerebral and obsessed by grand theory, she was practical and straightforward. Where he was confident to the point of hubris, she was often nervous and insecure. Where he was cool, she was warm. Where he had been a soft Quebec nationalist, she was a Red Tory.

They did, however, share a very important thing in common: they were both committed to cultural nationalism. MacDonald felt, like Masse, that culture was fundamental to the identity of the country. She felt, as well, that it was important to exempt culture from the free trade deal and to pursue the film policy that Masse had not been able to move forward.

In fact, very shortly after she began, she decided that a feature film policy would be her first priority. Considerable work had already been done on the subject as part of the preparations of Masse's brick on cultural sovereignty. The recommendations in that paper had been based, in part, on the work of an independent Film Industry Task Force that had proposed a relatively radical overhaul of both the financing and distribution of movies in Canada.

During the deliberations on the brick, cabinet had thrown Masse a sop by way of some cash to finance the production of movies, but had expressed no enthusiasm for the scheme he had proposed to license distributors and regulate what they could and could not distribute. The cabinet had been advised that limiting the ability of the US major studios to distribute films in Canada would engender a very hostile reaction.

MacDonald's first public act came very shortly after her appointment. In July 1986, she announced the creation of a $33-million Feature Film and Dubbing Fund. She did not touch on the issue of distribution, but noted that the new money was only "an important first step."[6]

What she did not tell the film moguls and mavens that had assembled for the announcement was that she had been to cabinet the month before, proposing the licensing system — and that it had been agreed upon, subject only to the proviso that the draft legislation come back to cabinet for ratification. Subsequently, however, the policy came under heavy attack from multiple sources within the government. To counter the backsliding, she wrote to her colleagues in November, reminding that the policy had been agreed at cabinet, summarizing its benefits and asking for their continued support.

The opponents included senior officials in finance, external affairs and the Privy Council Office, as well as the lead trade negotiator, Simon Reisman, and the ambassador to the United States, Allan Gotlieb. They feared that the policy would undermine the negotiations on the free trade agreement. In a cable from Washington, Gotlieb said that the introduction of the legislation "is likely to prove controversial in the United States. Timing could not possibly be worse given delicate stage in comprehensive trade [negotiations] and muscle flexing in Democratic congress."[7]

In order to pre-empt further whining from the trade officials, MacDonald decided to announce the bones of the policy in a speech at the Sutton Place hotel in Toronto early in 1987. Many of the people in attendance — film producers and distributors — had been lobbying the government for this very policy for a long time. Some were so moved by the announcement after so many years of frustration that they burst into tears.

The strategy behind the bill was very different from Baie-Comeau. Rather than being dreamt up in the minister's office, it had been put together by the department in conjunction with the industry. Kinsman had worked with the charming Daniel Weinzweig, then the head of the Canadian film distributors association. Daniel was a prince of Canadian cultural royalty. His father was John Weinzweig, the distinguished modernist composer; his mother was Helen Weinzweig, the Governor General's Award–nominated author. He himself ran a distribution company, specializing in art house and independent films.

The new policy tried to ensure that some proportion of foreign films would be distributed by Canadians, without forcing any divestiture of American assets. It required that films that were not owned by the major US studios be made available to Canadian distributors. Those films that the majors owned — that is, those that they had financed (50 per cent of the negative cost) or in which they owned worldwide rights — could continue to be distributed in Canada by them. As the minister had noted in her letter to her colleagues, the policy had "been carefully structured to escape any complaint of expropriation of property and does not deny any non-Canadian the right to operate in Canada."[8]

This seemed eminently fair. The US studios got to keep and distribute what was theirs, while independent films — whether from the US or elsewhere — would be subject to a new regime in which Canadian distributors would bid for their Canadian rights. The bidding system was designed to ensure that the independents received a fair price. It was estimated that this would repatriate 20 per cent of the Canadian box office, making significantly greater resources available for the production and promotion of Canadian movies. It did not go nearly as far as the *Broadcasting Act*, but it was a good step in expanding the garden to film.

To ensure that the American major studios were not blindsided and understood that their interests had been respected, Kinsman was sent to Los Angeles to explain the policy. Kinsman got a lesson in just how much Hollywood considered Canada an indivisible part of its market. Certainly that was the view of the studios' lobbying arm, the Motion Picture Association of America, whose longtime president was the notoriously powerful Jack Valenti, and whose chairman at the time was Frank Wells.

Kinsman met with Wells, the head of Disney, and with the distribution presidents of Warner Bros., Fox, Universal, MGM and Frank Mancuso, the chairman and CEO of Paramount.

The meetings were candid: The American studio executives made clear that they strenuously objected to the policy. The reporting telegram on Kinsman's foray from the Canadian embassy in Washington noted that the majors' strategy was "to speak with one voice behind

Valenti . . . in showing their adamant opposition to new policy which they find quote unacceptable, protectionist and with serious consequences for their business internationally unquote." The telegram went on to note that the majors had threatened reprisals and singled out the trade negotiations as an "area where [they] could apply pressure on the U.S. government."[9]

In the case of Frank Wells, he did not meet Kinsman in his office. To remind him of his place in the order of things, he met him in the cafeteria. Wells listened. He said that he understood the Canadian position perfectly and that he would do the same thing if he were us. After Kinsman left, he called Valenti and told him to kill the bill.

Jack Valenti had an enormous office in Washington. On entering, it was hard not to notice a photograph on a ledge near the left hand wall. It was positioned to give the impression that it was nothing but a souvenir; but it was impossible to miss. It was a picture of Lyndon Johnson taking the oath of office on Air Force One after the assassination of President Kennedy. Jackie was standing beside him, wearing the blood-stained dress. Two rows back, watching Johnson being sworn in, was Jack Valenti.

His power in Washington was legendary. He buttressed it with weekly showings for important politicians of major Hollywood pictures that had not yet been released. He screened the movies in a small theatre attached to his office, and then provided an excellent dinner in his private dining room. Senators, congressmen and cabinet secretaries showed up for his soirées, which almost always were attended by the movie stars themselves. He was the first person to see how the glamour of Hollywood could be used to exercise power in Washington.

Valenti's task of advancing the interests of the major studios was made easier by the presence of Ronald Reagan in the White House. Reagan had made his career in Hollywood and become president of the Screen Actors Guild. Hollywood was his home. Anything that threatened to compromise or defile it was anathema.

According to Reagan's staffers, it was one of the few subjects that could really raise the Gipper's ire. "You'll think he's dozing through a cabinet meeting and suddenly he'll sit up and deliver a lecture on how the Canadians are trying to screw up the film business."[10] Jack Valenti had no difficulty winding him up.

For Valenti, the Canadian film bill was not just a problem in itself. It was also a dangerous precedent that other countries might cite if Ottawa was allowed to get away with it. The important thing was to stop the disease before it could infect the rest of the world.

When Reagan came to Ottawa for an official meeting, Mulroney tried to move him on the subject, but without any success. He said to the president: "What if the Russians had 97 per cent of the screen time in the U.S. and Hollywood 3 per cent? Wouldn't you try to react?"[11]

It is not clear whether Reagan felt slighted to be compared to the Russians; but whatever his reaction, Mulroney's lobbying fell on deaf ears.

Meanwhile, Valenti was appearing everywhere to denounce the film bill. He worked the Congress in Washington; he leaned on the US trade negotiators not to go soft; he gave press conferences in Ottawa, explaining that the bill was simple theft. He debated with MacDonald, who boxed his ears.

Valenti's relentless lobbying seemed to stall the bill. MacDonald kept saying that it was coming, but it never appeared. Months passed and there was nothing.

As the film debate unfolded, the free trade negotiations continued. At the communications department, we produced a cabinet paper on the "cultural exemption." It explained the background to the issue, why it was important, what the prime minister had already said and how it would help sell the deal when it was finally concluded.

As far as the mechanics of the cultural exemption were concerned, it simply said that the cultural industries should not be part of it in any way. They were "off the table."

The exemption did not require that the Americans agree with the legitimacy of the Canadian measures; they were simply outside the purview of the agreement. This simple approach was designed to shelter the existing Canadian cultural-support measures while not creating precedents that the Americans could not live with.

The requirement for an exemption was being forcibly pushed not just by the artistic community in Toronto, but also by a coalition of the CEOs of the biggest media companies. Encouraged by Pierre Juneau — who was now president of the CBC — they lobbied the government to make sure that it did not give away the protections that they enjoyed.

For his part, Juneau, as head of a crown corporation, did not feel that it would be appropriate to lobby. Instead, he made it his business to explain the situation as best he could to the Americans. In a speech at Harvard of remarkable eloquence, he said, "Because of our brittle sense of nationhood, culture and identity have become somewhat synonymous. Our view is that culture is what a country says to itself, and about itself, to others, whatever the technique of expression may be: theatre, film and television, novels, recorded entertainment, painting, architecture or ballet. It is what makes a people interesting, worthy of attention by the rest of the world. It is how people of a country express their dreams and hopes, and how they talk about their past and their future. It is what they care about."[12]

Throughout all this, the departments of finance, external affairs and the Privy Council Office (the prime minister's department; not to be confused with his political office) continued implacably to oppose the film bill and the cultural exemption. They feared that they could scuttle the overall deal.

The prime minister talked to MacDonald about both matters a number of times. He suggested that she stop pushing the cultural exemption. On three separate occasions she threatened to resign. Without her insistence and toughness, there would not have been a cultural exemption. It may be the signal accomplishment during her time as minister.[13]

Eventually, the film bill and the free trade negotiations became entwined at the highest levels. With negotiations drawing to a close on all the larger items, it remained to be determined what to do about culture. The matter was apparently concluded with Reagan phoning Mulroney and saying simply that he could have the free trade deal or the film bill. The prime minister was left with no choice.

The last order of business was the cultural exemption. Since it was a reasonably elegant compromise, it was accepted by both sides, but with a significant amendment by the Americans. They argued that if culture was off the table and not part of the deal, then it also could not enjoy any of the protections in the deal. This meant that in future, if the US did not like a Canadian cultural initiative, it retained the right to "countervail" it by imposing penalties on any other part of the Canadian economy.

Jack Valenti claimed credit for the amendment. But whatever the source, the principal negotiator for the US — Peter Murphy — understood its value. He said, "The Canadians in a sense didn't get it . . . Because the way the agreement is written, if there's a problem, the U.S. will take action — and it doesn't have to show injury . . . The retaliatory possibilities are huge."[14] There it was. The Canadians got the exemption, but it protected almost nothing. If they stepped out of line in the cultural area, the Americans could punish them anywhere they liked — over steel, cattle, farm machinery, computer parts, anything at all.

The free trade negotiations were concluded in the fall of 1987 and came into force in January 1989. Even after the deal was finished, MacDonald continued to insist that the film legislation was still in the works. In early 1988, she tabled a watered-down bill in the House of Commons. It never got beyond first reading and died when an election was called later in the year.

The free trade agreement was the central issue in that campaign. The Liberals under John Turner campaigned against it. The Conservatives were returned with a second majority government. MacDonald lost her seat. Masse won his and even became minister of communications a second time, but he was a spent force. He continued to press his arguments on cultural sovereignty; nobody in the cabinet listened and he was once again shuffled to a portfolio where he could cause no trouble.

Between them, Masse and MacDonald had boldly proposed structural change for the cultural industries, a major expansion of the garden. Their efforts yielded extremely mixed results.

The Baie-Comeau policy was a mess from the beginning. It failed and was ultimately killed. The Canadian publishing industry remained weak and poorly capitalized. Over the years, the remaining major Canadian-owned houses were either consumed by foreigners or went bankrupt. As of 2019 the only surviving Canadian-owned and -controlled companies are small and they struggle constantly to survive.

The film policy, although much better conceived, met a similar fate. It was killed not by its own inadequacies, but by the objections of the most powerful people in the United States and the Canadian government's determination to conclude the free trade agreement. It has never been revived, with the result that the Canadian film business remains, like the book business, a sort of hobby farm. Canadian films get financed and distributed (sort of), but their performance remains anaemic. They do not do much better at the domestic box office than they did in the 1980s.

The free trade negotiations also made clear, once again, that the Americans do not care about direct subsidies to Canadian culture. They are perfectly happy for the Canadian government to spend as much as it likes — whether in tax credits, equity investments or direct grants — subsidizing the production of anything: books, movies, TV shows, whatever. Subsidies do not disturb the control of their companies over the means of distribution.

The efforts of Marcel Masse, Flora MacDonald and the officials at the Department of Communications to carve out a cultural policy with real teeth would not come again. Thirty years later, their tenures mark the most ambitious program of national self-assertion since the passage of the 1968 *Broadcasting Act* by the Pearson government. It is a shame that the efforts took place while the government was negotiating the free trade agreement. In the absence of those negotiations, the Americans would have had much less leverage and the policies could well have come to fruition.

The incomplete legacies of Marcel Masse and Flora MacDonald haunt us still.

CHAPTER 4

Watering the Garden: The Chrétien Liberals

Having enjoyed the greatest victory in Canadian history in 1983, the Conservatives were handed the most crushing defeat in Canadian history by Jean Chrétien ten years later. They were reduced to two seats. Their loss had nothing to do with anything cultural. Canadians, as is their habit, just get fed up with almost any government after a decade and throw it out.

With the transfer of power to the Liberals, there was no attempt to expand the garden to books and movies. They did, however, continue to maintain the garden for television.

In the early 1990s, new American direct-to-home satellites began broadcasting. Their footprints fell over the most populated areas of Canada, allowing Canadians that had the necessary decoding equipment to access the signals. The direct-to-home providers offered a plethora of US TV services that were not licensed in Canada. The garden wall, it appeared, had once again been breached.

Canadian cable companies and broadcasters, seeing the perils involved for their businesses, branded the new satellites "Death Stars" and began a concerted campaign to have them de-weaponized, and to have the garden restored.

The government acted expeditiously. It appointed a panel of three "wise men," including the previously shunned Robert Rabinovitch, to advise on what to do. In three months, the trio produced a report that said the CRTC should license Canadian alternatives and ban the US ones. The government ordered the commission to do so and the matter was resolved.

It is striking how the Chrétien Liberals responded to the incursion of the foreign satellites into the garden. The matter was studied, a report issued, a discussion held, a decision made and the problem all resolved within half a year. It stands in marked contrast to the Justin Trudeau Liberals' inability to figure out how to deal with the incursion of the FAANGs. As of early 2019, it had gone on almost four years with no end in sight.

During the course of the 1990s, the government also moved to water the flowers in the garden and improve the financing of Canadian TV. In 1994, the CRTC established the Cable Production Fund. It was the result of a clever, although slightly cynical, deal made between the commission and the cable industry.

In those days, cable rates were supposed to go down once operators had completed paying for certain capital expenditures. The cable folks suggested that rather than see their revenues fall, they would split the difference, keeping half of what they would otherwise lose and giving the rest to a fund that would finance Canadian TV shows. The "rest" in question was 5 per cent of their gross revenues. The CRTC agreed, providing a gift to both the cable and independent production industries. In 1996, the Cable Production Fund was combined with Telefilm's Broadcast Fund, which Francis Fox had begun, to create the Canadian Television Fund. The fund focussed on the most expensive and hardest to finance shows: drama, comedies, documentaries, children's shows and the performing arts.

Contributions to the fund from the cable and satellite companies rose from $46 million in 1997 to $86 million in 2000.[1] Combined with money from the federal government, the fund had revenues of over $180 million in 2000.[2]

During this period, I had the honour of chairing the board of the fund. One of the most interesting problems we had was how to manage the demand for the ever increasing amounts of money. No matter how much there was in the pot, there was never enough to finance all the shows that wanted access to it.

Over the course of a number of meetings, we decided to tighten the eligibility criteria substantially. First, we forced the broadcasters to contribute more to the financing of the shows. Then, we decided that they would all have to be 10/10s, with full Canadian creative teams attached. Finally, we put in rules requiring that the programs be "distinctively" Canadian. We insisted that they be clearly shot and set in Canada, have Canadian characters and explore Canadian themes and stories.

Not surprisingly, there was anguished moaning from the Canadian TV producers. Forcing the shows to be 10/10 meant it was impossible to stuff an American writer or an American star into the creative team. Worse still, the distinctiveness requirements would make it much harder, possibly impossible, to sell the show in the United States. Whatever their other merits, Americans do not like their TV and movies to be about anybody but themselves.

After I left the chairmanship of the fund, the distinctiveness tests were rolled back. Apparently the notion that

Canadian taxpayers' money should be spent on making shows that looked and felt Canadian was a cultural bridge too far. It was the last and only time a truly cultural test had been used to decide what got funded.

As the fund evolved, it changed its name to the Canada Media Fund to reflect the fact that it supported not just television shows but digital audio-visual products as well. It also continued to grow as the revenues of the cable companies continued to increase throughout the 1990s.

In 1995, the government created a system of tax credits to further subsidize TV and film production. They replaced a somewhat shambolic system of tax shelters that had been available in the 1980s.

Despite their name, tax credits have nothing to do with tax. Rather they are cash subsidies, pure and simple. The name "tax credits" was probably chosen to make them sound less like straight cash transfers and more like the sorts of benefits that are given to other industries. They are very simple in their operation. When a film or TV show is completed, the producer sends a cost report to the Canadian Audio-Visual Certification Office, a division of the Department of Canadian Heritage. Once the cost reports have been verified, the producer receives a cheque for a certain portion of the labour expense associated with the production.

The tax credits provide support to a broader array of TV shows than the Canadian Media Fund, including lifestyle, cooking and home renovation shows. They can, as well, be combined with the subsidies from the Canadian Media Fund to finance dramas and documentaries, which are much more expensive. News and sports shows do not qualify.

There are no caps on the value of these credits. The costs to the government depend on the level of demand; the more shows that are made that qualify, the more it costs the treasury. The value of the credits increased from $6 million in 1995 to over $170 million in 2000.[3]

By the end of the decade, the tax credits and the Canadian Media Fund dollars combined were worth almost $350 million per year.

The CRTC complemented the new subsidies by requiring the Canadian broadcasters to buy and schedule Canadian shows. In the early days, this took the form of quotas. Later on, the commission required broadcasters to spend a certain proportion of their gross revenues on Canadian shows. For the biggest conventional broadcasters — CTV, Global and Citytv — it was 30 per cent, at least 5 per cent of which had to be spent on the hard-to-finance shows for which the Canadian Media Fund was established (drama, etc.).[4]

As the Canadian broadcasting system evolved and as specialty/cable channels (the 600-channel universe) began to emerge, the CRTC, by and large, continued to pursue the garden strategy. Very few US channels were allowed to be picked up by the Canadian cable companies and distributed in Canada. Those that were — CNN and A&E — had to be "tiered" with the new Canadian specialty channels to give "lift" to the latter.

The Canadian channels themselves were often Canadianized versions of US ones, using American shows to help subsidize their purely Canadian ones. Over the course of the 1980s, the CRTC licensed twenty new Canadian pay and specialty channels; thirty more were greenlit in the 1990s. By the year 2000, there were almost a hundred of them.[5]

The Canadian TV business flourished. The garden strategy had worked exceptionally well. Combined with the tax credits and the money from the Canadian Media Fund, the industry grew and expanded. In 2000, the private Canadian television industry had revenues of more than $3 billion per year and employed over 11,000 people. Around this time, CBC TV had revenues of almost $1.3 billion from advertising and the Parliamentary appropriation, and employed almost 10,000 people.[6]

The government also moved to shore up the magazine business. It reconfigured a postal subsidy predating Confederation into a direct cash subsidy to the magazine industry. Known as the Canada Periodical Fund, it provides $75 million per year in assistance.

The newspaper business also expanded and flourished.

The venerable Southam chain that consisted of the most important broadsheets in the largest markets — the *Ottawa Citizen*, Vancouver's the *Province*, the *Calgary Herald*, Montreal's the *Gazette* and others — churned out a steady stream of reliable earnings. So too did the Torstar group, the owners of the *Toronto Star* and a raft of smaller papers. Even the independents — the *Chronicle Herald* and the *Winnipeg Free Press* — did well financially.

The business was so buoyant that competitors began to emerge. The *Toronto Sun*, a tabloid paper, emphasizing sports, crime, conservative politics and large-breasted women (the Sunshine Girl) started in 1971. It was followed by the creation of the *Edmonton Sun* in 1978, the *Calgary Sun* in 1980, the *Ottawa Sun* in 1988 and finally the *Winnipeg Sun*. Eventually, the *Sun* chain operated in competition with the Southam broadsheets in all the largest cities of English Canada, except Vancouver.

The *Sun* titles, too, generated stable and robust profits. Paul Godfrey, the head of the chain in the late 1990s, used to joke that the *Toronto Sun* made so much money in those days that even he, Paul Godfrey, "could not screw it up."

In 1996, Conrad Black, the international newspaper tycoon, historian, gadfly, future felon, egomaniac and owner of the venerable *Telegram* in the UK, bought the Southam chain. His plan was to use it to help create and finance a new national paper to compete with the *Globe and Mail*. Two years later, he launched the *National Post*, the first new national paper to be created in decades.

The *Post* was a revelation. It emphasized long — sometimes very long — expository pieces, clever right-wing commentary and witty articles by journalists who knew how to write. Under its first great editor, Ken Whyte, the paper brought real competition to the grey and dull *Globe and Mail*.

In 2000, the newspaper business was doing very well. The papers were fat with ads. The classifieds were where everyone went to find work, housing, lost cats and automobiles. The grocery and department stores stuffed the papers with flyers, sales notices and special deals. Each day's edition landed on the front doorstep with a satisfying thud. On Saturdays, they swelled to the size of telephone books, full of multiple sections and endless ads. The combined revenues of the newspapers was $4.7 billion and they had profits of almost $700 million.[7]

They also exercised immense political and cultural power. Politicians, special pleaders, trade associations, charities and interest groups of one variety or another all craved their attention and coverage. Along with TV news, newspapers were the most effective and reliable way of communicating with the Canadian public. Good coverage could make a career; bad coverage could destroy it.

In 2000, the Southam group was bought by Canwest. The company's founder, Israel "Izzy" Asper — a noted jazz enthusiast, tax lawyer, bon vivant and sometime politician

— had already built its Global TV assets into one of Canada's largest broadcasting groups, with operations in almost all the major cities in the country. He had expanded internationally, with services in Australia, New Zealand, Chile and Ireland, and production facilities in Los Angeles. It was one of the biggest broadcasting groups in the world.

Asper bought the newspapers as part of a fashionable strategy to create "converged" media assets. The notion was that there were synergies to be had by owning common types of content. The newspapers could help feed and promote the TV news and vice versa; advertising could be bundled and sold across platforms, creating richer offers for advertisers; and back offices could be rationalized, producing savings in the finance, human resource and executive departments. Asper paid a heady price for Conrad Black's group of papers, but justified it on the basis that newspapers overall were doing well.

Inspired by Canwest, a "convergence" play was also pursued by Bell when it bought the CTV group, along with its specialty channels (TSN, RDS, Discovery and Viewer's Choice) for $2.3 billion later that year.[8] The Bell strategy differed significantly, however, since it was not converging content assets, but twinning carriage with content. The president of Bell, Jean Monty, believed that there were synergies available in putting together the very different businesses of TV and telecommunications.

This strategy had also proven popular in the US. In a moment of extraordinary optimism, AOL offered to buy Time Warner, one of the biggest content owners and cable companies, in a mega-deal for $164 billion US. Eventually the two merged in a complex new structure that proved enormously unsuccessful. Two years after consummation of the deal, the new company wrote down $99 billion US in goodwill. It was the largest write down in US history.

The success of convergence strategies would prove check- ered at best, coming in and out of favour as the years went by. The next decade would see an unwinding of its strategy by Bell and then a recommitment. The same was to be true of the Shaws. The fate of mergers between the various differ- ent types of media companies would dominate the Canadian business landscape for the next twenty years.

In 2006, CTV bought the CHUM group, which included two TV networks, Citytv and the A channels, a provincial educational channel, twenty specialty networks (including MuchMusic and Space) and thirty-three radio stations for $1.7 billion.[9] Although Bell itself declined to participate in the purchase and saw its position watered down in CTV, it nevertheless demonstrated the market's confidence in the value of traditional TV assets.

For its part, Canwest's new CEO, Leonard Asper, added to his father's empire by buying Alliance Atlantis with an affiliate of Goldman Sachs in 2007. Together they paid $1.5 billion for thirteen high-quality specialty channels that included HGTV, History Television, the Food Channel and Showcase. Canwest now owned the Global TV empire, the *National Post* and the Southam chain, along with its new clutch of specialty networks. It had placed a huge bet on the success of convergence.[10]

In acquiring Alliance Atlantis, Canwest added to the very large debt burden that it was already carrying. Nevertheless, the Canadian financial markets were happy to make significant funds available, as were extremely sophisticated international players like Goldman Sachs. Everyone believed strongly in the value of these assets.

The late 1990s and early 2000s were halcyon years for Canadian media, a veritable golden age.

In early 2000, the Liberal government began pumping more money into the big cultural agencies. Perhaps excited by the general optimism of the times, the government also took another kick at feature films. Rather than trying to revive Flora MacDonald's film bill, the Liberals and their energetic heritage minister, Sheila Copps, decided simply to inject $100 million into Telefilm and set a target: Canadian films would get 5 per cent of the domestic box office.

Shortly after the government's announcement about its new Feature Film Fund, I was asked if I would be interested in becoming the CEO of Telefilm. During the course of our discussions, we talked at length about the 5 per cent target. Without changes like those championed by Flora MacDonald, it seemed a daunting challenge. The film industry remained outside the garden.

I made it clear that I did not disagree with the target. Box office sales were a reasonable measure of success; there is no point making films that nobody sees or wants to see. Movies, after all, are both an art and a form of popular entertainment. They flourish in the sun of popular regard.

It was clear, however, that the Liberals had no intention of resurrecting the film bill. Doubtless they were not much interested in suffering the wrath of the Americans. Accepting the job meant, therefore, trying to get to 5 per cent with nothing more than money to assist the process. Crossing my fingers and letting hope triumph over better judgement, I said yes.

When I arrived at Telefilm in 2002, it was apparent that nothing had been done to change any of the policies of the past in the direction of the 5 per cent goal. The French side was doing quite well, but the English side was a graveyard of unwatched and unloved films about unhappy families, with downbeat plots and sad endings. They had won a few prizes at international competitions, but the Canadian public did not seem to care and they withered at the box office.

Part of the problem, as Masse and MacDonald had seen, was the relative weakness of the Canadian distributors. They were poorly capitalized, living in most cases on a knife edge, too poor to participate effectively in the financing or promotion of the films they bought. In fact, the policies of the period made it more profitable for them not to release films theatrically, but simply to sell them to the TV companies willing to buy them.

The great exception was Alliance Atlantis Releasing, the distribution arm of Alliance Atlantis Films. Run by Victor Loewy since the mid-1980s, it had made deals to distribute independent films. Its most important agreement was with New Line Cinema, which produced the *Lord of the Rings* trilogy, whose first picture in 2001 was a smash hit. It also had deals with Quentin Tarantino for *Pulp Fiction* and others for everything from *Teenage Mutant Ninja Turtles* to *Dumb and Dumber*.

The success of these films at the Canadian box office made it possible for Alliance Atlantis to support many of the most important Canadian films ever made. It participated in: David Cronenberg's *eXistenZ* and *A History of Violence*; Atom Egoyan's *The Sweet Hereafter*; and Denys Arcand's *The Barbarian Invasions*, which won the Oscar for best foreign language picture in 2003. Alliance Atlantis proved, in fact, that Masse and MacDonald had been right.

Alliance Atlantis aside, however, the distribution of English Canadian films was more a scam than a business. To get financing for production from Telefilm, a producer had to have a Canadian distributor attached to the project. This took the form of a "guarantee" paid to the producer. The guarantee entitled the distributor to sell the film in Canada to movie houses, TV channels, video-on-demand services (VOD), premium pay-TV (the Movie Network) and home video (DVD) retailers. The distributor's role was to market the film, pay for the prints and promote it to ensure its financial success.

The problem was that the "guarantees" were always too small. They could be recouped by the distributor simply selling the movie to TV, VOD and DVD, while making a small profit. The costs of releasing to movie houses was always substantial and risky, without any assurance that the distributor could recover those costs, let alone make any money. In fact, the track record for most English Canadian films at the domestic box office was so poor that it was not surprising that distributors were afraid of releasing them theatrically.

To satisfy Telefilm's requirements that the films it financed be released in Canadian movie houses, the distributors would often "four wall" them. Four walling involved renting a cinema somewhere in the country and then showing the film without any promotion. That way, the distributor avoided all the highly risky costs involved in a real theatrical release and kept the profits made from selling it to TV. This, of course, meant that the film was not effectively released at all. It was hardly a surprise, therefore, that English Canadian film failed so badly at the box office.

To rectify the problem, it was decided that Telefilm would not finance any movies unless their distributors were really "at risk." This meant they had to guarantee that they would spend a minimum amount of money on prints and advertising for the theatrical release of the movies they "guaranteed." This would force the distributors to pick up only those films that they genuinely believed would succeed at the box office and ensure that they got properly distributed. In the absence of a film bill, it was the best idea I had to break the distribution problem and make a tentative start on a garden for Canadian movies.

The reaction was instantaneous and overwhelmingly negative. The producers feared that the distributors would never step up and that their films would not get made. The distributors were too poor to be comfortable with risk, and feared that one or two bad decisions under the new rules would bankrupt them.

The rules were released on the eve of the annual Cannes Film Festival. A large number of Canadian film producers and distributors were already in Cannes when they learned about the new approach. There were cries of outrage and disbelief.

I received a call from the head of the producers association as I was preparing to leave for the festival.

"It's very bad over here," she said. "There is a lot of dark talk."

"Dark talk?" I asked.

"Yes. Threats are being made."

"Threats?"

I did not know the film community very well. I had no idea what kinds of threats they might be making. Were they planning to physically attack me? Denounce me to the press and demand my resignation? Call me a name?

"Yes, threats."

"What kind of threats?"

"They are threatening to not attend your cocktail party!"

The new policy held and Telefilm proceeded to finance only those films where the distributor was genuinely at risk. It improved the performance at the box office somewhat, but it was no substitute for the film bill that MacDonald had wanted. While Canadian movies took 5.3 per cent of Canada's domestic cinema revenues in 2005, a dramatic improvement over the 2 per cent that had been typical for the previous three decades, it was largely a result of the extraordinary success of Quebec films that year. The 5 per cent has never been achieved since and performance at the box office has collapsed in recent years to historic lows.[11]

It was sobering to realize that even with the injection of substantial new money into the financing of Canadian films and an aggressive approach with the Canadian distributors, very little was accomplished. It appeared that unless the garden strategy was pursued for movies, the Canadian industry would continue to languish.

CHAPTER 5

The Garden Invaded: The Harper Years

In 2006, the government changed again. The Liberals gave way to the Conservatives under Stephen Harper. They were a different crew altogether. Many of them came from small-town and suburban ridings, carrying with them the traditional resentment of Canada's big cities. They actively disliked Montreal and Toronto, with their snobby, champagne-swilling cultural elites.

In an unguarded moment, Stephen Harper captured the attitude of the new government. After announcing $45 million in cuts to the arts early in his mandate, he said, "I think when ordinary working people come home, turn on the TV and see a bunch of people at, you know, a rich gala subsidized by taxpayers, claiming their subsidies are not high enough . . . I'm not sure that resonates with ordinary people."[1]

This was a curious charge to be made by a man who was subsidized with a house at 24 Sussex, a bulletproof limousine, a cottage on Meech Lake and a substantial salary.

The new government's contempt for culture expressed itself not just in cuts to the big cultural agencies, but also in the ministers they appointed to represent them, the boards they appointed to supervise them and the endless attacks they made on them to placate their "base." Rather than attempting to resurrect the cultural ambitions of the Mulroney government, the Harper version of the Tories pursued a policy of malign neglect.

The ministers of heritage were exemplars of the approach. The first, Bev Oda, evinced so little interest in her portfolio that she inspired a letter-writing campaign by one of Canada's most famous novelists, the Man Booker Prize winner, Yann Martel.

He recalled being invited to sit in the public galleries at the House of Commons to hear the government's tribute to the fiftieth anniversary of the Canada Council. What he heard appalled him. Bev Oda droned out a very short statement in an exhausted monotone. The prime minister, sitting close to her on the front benches, never looked up, as though preoccupied with other matters or consumed by indifference. Watching them, Martel wondered why they seemed so bored. He later wrote that "he [Harper] sounds and governs like one who cares little for the arts."[2]

In response, Martel began what he described as the "loneliest book club in the world." Every two weeks, he sent the prime minister a book with a covering letter explaining why he should read it. He hoped to help Harper "understand that Canadian books, films, music and other cultural enterprises exist not as mere entertainment alongside the real business of making money, but as 'the various elements that make up the sum total of Canadian civilization.'"[3]

Over the course of four years, he sent the prime minister a hundred books and letters. Harper never replied to any of them.

A good example of the Conservatives' general attitude to culture was its treatment of the CBC, Canada's largest

and most important cultural institution. It was their favou-
rite target for fundraising from their base. The head of
the party, Doug Finley, would regularly send out letters
to the party membership explaining the hopeless bias of
the CBC's news, how it was full of secret Liberals, how
the only thing that stood between the faithful and the dark
conspiracies of the corporation was the Conservative Party.
He would then urge them to send money to the party to
keep the pollution of the CBC at bay.

"Worked like a charm," Finley told me. "Attacking the
CBC was the best fundraising tool. Never failed," he said
with a laugh.

The new government also stuffed the board of the corporation with Tory bag men and time servers, true believers
in the iniquity of the corporation. None of them seemed to
know or care about Canadian culture.

In November 2007, the government named Hubert T.
Lacroix to a five-year term as president of the CBC. He was
an extraordinary choice. Lacroix had no significant management experience. In fact, it was not clear that he had ever
run anything bigger than a bath. Now he was in charge of
a media company with almost 10,000 full- and part-time
employees.

Throughout their tenures, the new board and the new president managed to confuse the interests of the Conservative
Party with their duty to the corporation. Although the board
members had been reminded that their responsibility was
first and foremost to the interests of the CBC, they never
stood up to protect Canada's largest cultural institution in
the face of endless attacks from the government.

One day during all this unpleasantness, I sat down to have
lunch with Flora MacDonald and seek her counsel.

"Why do your people hate the CBC so much?" I asked.

"My people?" she replied.

"Yes. Your people, your party, the Conservative Party."

"They are not my people. They are a different party from the one I was in."

"But you must have some insight into why they hate the CBC so much."

"Oh, Richard," she laughed. "Don't think that you're special. They hate everything."

"Everything?"

"Yes, everything. That's what they do. They are haters."

And she was right. They hated all the cultural agencies. The CBC was not special. The policy of malign neglect was applied everywhere: Boards were stacked with hostile Tories and non-entities were appointed to senior positions.

The most egregious example of political abuse happened after I had left the CBC. The then head of the French news department, Alain Saulnier, was called before the board to do a post-mortem of the coverage of the 2011 election. The Conservatives had lost a significant number of seats in Quebec. It was widely believed that a good part of the reason was the prime minister's denigrating remarks about the cultural community at "rich galas subsidized by taxpayers." That, however, was not the view of the CBC board.

The meeting began badly. Members of the board, Pierre Gingras and Remi Racine, demanded to know whether Saulnier understood why the Conservatives had lost so many seats in Quebec. Without pausing for reply, Gingras explained that the loss was a result of the biased coverage that Saulnier and his team had produced. They lost because the CBC's French arm had slanted the news to advantage the Liberals and disadvantage the Tories.[4]

This was all drivel. The French news department, like its English counterpart, always did extensive, independent studies during election campaigns to ensure that the coverage of all parties was fair and balanced. The studies showed that this was indeed the case this time around. But they were of no comfort to the rabid members of the board, who spent the better part of two hours working over Saulnier. While the auto-da-fé was going on, neither the acting head of French services nor the president objected.

Shortly thereafter, Saulnier was dismissed. Having proved that they could get the news department under control, the acting head of French services became the permanent head, and Lacroix was rewarded with another five-year term as president of the CBC. Nobody in the history of the corporation had ever received two full terms before.[5]

While the Conservatives were attacking the CBC and the financing of culture generally, the FAANGs were beginning to enter the Canadian market in force.

They entered the garden through the tiniest hole.

In 1999, the CRTC looked into the question of "new media." The *Broadcasting Act* of 1991 had updated the definition of "broadcasting" to make clear that it covered any transmission of pictures and sound to the general public by whatever means, including the internet. The commission wanted to know whether the emerging digital content was, in fact, broadcasting and fell within its jurisdiction.

In those long ago days, the internet ran mostly on dial-up telephone lines. It was extremely slow and cumbersome. The cable industry and the telephone companies were just beginning to experiment with higher-speed modems. The principal use of the internet was for e-mail.

The biggest and most sophisticated digital platform was

America Online (AOL). It offered access to the internet and a collection of very simple applications that ran largely through chat rooms. These included educational services, along with simple news, weather and homework help.

When the CRTC considered the "new media" of the period, it determined that although some of the "new media" were technically broadcasters under the *Act*, there did not seem to be much point regulating them, since they had no impact on the broadcasting system. In 1999, it was hard to quibble with this reasoning.

The commission, therefore, issued a Digital Media Exemption Order. The order meant that the emerging digital platforms were not subject to Canadian ownership rules, content quotas or requirements to contribute to the financing or distribution of Canadian culture in any way. They were free to do whatever they wanted.[6]

Facebook opened its platform to the general public in 2006. This marked the beginning of its colossal expansion. Within three years, it would have almost 500 million users worldwide. No media company had ever had so many customers; but the real growth was still to come.

For its part, Google had launched in 1998 and had been in the Canadian market for some time, offering its search engine and e-mail service. By 2007, it had bought Applied Semantics, Urchin Software and DoubleClick, all of which were merged into its ferociously effective advertising engine.

In 2007, it added YouTube, the extraordinarily successful platform that would dominate both amateur and short-form video. It is difficult to overstate how important YouTube would become to the emergence of a whole new generation of Canadian artists and performers. By way of example,

Lilly Singh, the rapper, comedian and personality from Scarborough, launched her YouTube channel in 2010. Seven years later, she had over 13 million subscribers and had received more than 2 billion views. To put this in perspective, a very successful Canadian drama on TV would be one that attracted more than a million viewers.

YouTube has also become central to the making and release of music videos. Drake's great hit "Hotline Bling" attracted over 1.3 billion views; Justin Bieber's "Sorry" netted almost 3 billion. These are staggering numbers, yet are not record holders. "Despacito" has been seen more than 5 billion times. In the past, platinum sales for an album meant that it sold more than a million copies. The best-selling albums of all time — *Thriller* and the Eagles' *Greatest Hits* — sold 29 million units each.

While Google and Facebook were beginning their rise to digital dominance, the financial markets came under significant strain. The collapse of the US housing bubble and its associated high-risk financial products in 2008 triggered a worldwide meltdown that led to the greatest recession since the Great Depression. Everywhere, revenues shrank, profits dried up, firms went bankrupt and unemployment soared.

The impact on the advertising markets was particularly brutal. In a flash, the sale of advertising seemed to fall off a cliff for both newspapers and TV.

At the time, I was still at the CBC. Once the fall began, it accelerated at a speed nobody had ever seen. I called friends at Global and CTV to find out if their experiences were the same. They told me that, if anything, their problems were worse. Their annual revenue targets were collapsing before their eyes. Their sales executives were in despair.

From 2008 to 2009, revenues fell 12 per cent for the newspapers and 9 per cent for TV. The newspaper advertising business never recovered.[7]

While the recession was underway, Google and Facebook continued to roll out new products. Google introduced Chrome, its web browser, in 2008. Ten years after its release, it had an almost two-thirds share of all web browsing worldwide. This meant that it could track individuals' visits to every website they went to, providing a very clear sense of what that person was interested in and what they might buy.

Google also introduced Android in 2008. The open-source, mobile operating system was designed to compete with Apple. It did so very successfully and is now the world's leader. Its dominance allowed Google to build proprietary systems on top of it, including the Android app store and Android TV. In 2017, just nine years after Android launched, its app store had recorded 94 billion installs.[8]

As the advertising markets were melting down for traditional media, Google and Facebook saw theirs continue to grow. While the traditional media were being hammered, digital advertising revenue grew to almost 20 per cent of the Canadian market.[9] This was a remarkable achievement. Normally, during severe economic downturns, marketing and advertising budgets are cut back to conserve cash. Google and Facebook managed to reverse the trend.

The reason for their success is not hard to understand; they solved the fundamental problem of attributing value to advertising.

The problem was most clearly stated for the first time by John Wanamaker (or perhaps Henry Ford or J.C. Penney, opinions differ): "Half of the money I spend on advertising is wasted; the trouble is I don't know which half."

There, in a nutshell, is the great dilemma of advertisers. The problem with buying ads in magazines, newspapers, TV or radio is that one does not know whether anyone has seen or heard the ads; and, if they did, who they were, whether the ad made any impact and, if so, whether it resulted in a purchase. This is often called the problem of "attribution." Did the ad result in a sale?

The big digital platforms of Google and Facebook have moved a very long way toward solving the attribution problem. They can verify that a potential customer saw an ad and acted on it.

How do they do this?

First, when ads are presented on digital platforms, they can be "clicked." This allows the advertiser to know that a potential customer actually saw the ad and was sufficiently interested to take action and explore the offer. One cannot "click" on radio, TV or newspaper ads.

For a time, however, the advertiser did not know who clicked. It could have been a child or a dog. There was no way of ascertaining that the clicker could be a bona-fide purchaser.

The trick was to be able to attribute the click to a real, identifiable person. This became possible when e-mail addresses started to be used as identifiers. Google, of course, knew who you were as soon as you signed up for e-mail or Chrome.

Facebook, by having users register with their e-mail addresses, also knows exactly who is doing what. It also knows who the person's friends are, what they like, whether they have dogs or children, where they travel — indeed, almost everything about their lives.

Now Google and Facebook can assure advertisers that their messages are getting through to real, identifiable people. By only charging if the real person clicks on the ad, they can also guarantee that the person saw the ad and found it sufficiently interesting to look at it in detail. If the clicked ad then leads to an online store and the goods are bought, the circle is complete. Wanamaker's problem is solved. The advertiser can directly attribute the sale to the ad.

But Google and Facebook can do much more. Because they know so much about their users and because there are so many — Google and Facebook have over 2 billion each — they have giant data sets (10–15 exabytes: 1 billion gigabytes) that they can analyze to build psychographic profiles of users, target potential buyers through extremely refined demographics or map where certain products are being bought and then tie the information back to the demographic and psychographic analyses.

The CRTC reviewed the appropriateness of extending its Digital Media Exemption Order in 2009. Despite the rise of Google and Facebook, the emergence of YouTube, and the collapse of the traditional advertising markets, the regulator declined to change its position. The exemption order was extended for another five years. As far as the CRTC was concerned, the new platforms still did not look like they had anything to do with traditional media. They were about searches and keeping in touch with friends and making amateur videos. The commission left the hole wide open, allowing the dog-strangling vines of digital media to take over more of the garden.[10]

The rise of digital advertising and the recession together proved too much for the Canwest empire. Its debt had become so great that the reduced revenues of the recession forced it to seek bankruptcy protection in 2009. The great experiment with "convergence" that Izzy Asper had initiated by buying Conrad Black's newspaper empire, and that had been continued by his son, Leonard, with the purchase of Alliance Atlantis, had come to an end, felled by debt and the biggest recession in the postwar period.

At the end of 2010, the Canadian advertising market strengthened. The collapse in newspaper revenue paused and TV advertising improved slightly. The banks and the traditional media executives did not conclude that the Aspers' fate reflected a structural shift in their businesses. Rather, they concluded that the Canadian media business still looked like a reasonable investment.

Sophisticated buyers began to spend heavily again to acquire traditional media.

In May of 2010, the Shaw family purchased the Canwest TV assets out of receivership for $2 billion. It acquired Global TV plus all of Canwest's specialty channels, including those they had purchased from Alliance Atlantis.[11] As the *Globe and Mail* noted admiringly, "With the purchase of the distressed assets of Canwest Global Communications Corp. from Goldman Sachs, the Shaws join mega-players CTV Globemedia Inc. and Rogers Communications Inc. in the major leagues of private media empires."[12]

Not to be outdone, Bell announced in the same year that it was buying back all of CTV and its specialty channels (TSN, etc.) for $1.3 billion.[13] George Cope, the president of BCE, in the incomparable management speak of large companies, explained his reasoning: "With video streaming rapidly growing in popularity among Canadians, who are increasingly moving to mobile, online and digital television platforms for video content, we need to acquire CTV's wide range of video content with the objective of enhancing the execution of our strategic imperatives by seeking to leverage our broadband network investments to accelerate video growth across all four screens — mobile smartphones and tablets, online and television — and to achieve a competitive cost structure."[14]

It appeared that convergence was back with a vengeance. Although Cope might not have known it at the time, his new convergence play positioned him as a potentially serious competitor to the new foreign TV streaming services that were beginning to emerge. Given its size and mix of assets, Bell might, just might, stand a chance against Netflix and the others that were waiting in the wings.

Bell doubled down on its bet in 2012 when it announced plans to buy Astral Media, which controlled a clutch of attractive French-language specialty channels plus the Movie Network and the rights to HBO in Canada. When Bell first applied to the CTRC to transfer the licences, it was turned down. The commission ruled that Bell would control too much of the Canadian TV market and enjoy too much power.

Bell proposed to sell off some of the TV and radio assets it would acquire with Astral and asked the CRTC a second time to let it proceed. This time the commission agreed. For the price of $3 billion, Bell became the largest owner of TV properties in Canada, with a 36 per cent share of viewing in the English market and a 23 per cent share of viewing in the French market.[15] It asserted the same rationale as it had for the CTV deal. Buying Astral would help Bell achieve its "strategic objectives."

By the beginning of 2010, all of Canwest's assets had been bought, typically by large telecommunications-based companies. Shaw (including Corus, which is controlled by the Shaw family), Rogers and Bell owned almost all the television networks in English Canada. This was an unprecedented level of concentration.

The year 2010 stands as the high water mark of Canadian media. The big groups were profitable. They were producing significant quantities of content that Canadians were consuming with increasing interest and attention. They were employing large numbers of people. Investors still found the businesses very attractive.

It was hard to believe that the FAANGs were about to pull down the entire edifice.

In 2010, Netflix entered the Canadian market. On the basis of a well-priced offer of attractive TV shows, it began to grow. From a standing start, it expanded into more than 10 per cent of Canadian households within two years. Its growth then accelerated. As of late 2018, it was found in approximately 50 per cent of Canadian households.[16]

To begin, Netflix offered old TV shows and movies. As time went on, however, it began to invest in original content. Its first major series was *House of Cards*, which cost an extraordinary $10 million per episode and enjoyed huge critical and popular success.

Buoyed by *House of Cards*, Netflix began to pour money into new, sometimes very expensive scripted series. Over the next few years, it financed *Orange Is the New Black*, *Narcos*, a reboot of *Gilmore Girls*, a collection of Marvel universe shows including *Daredevil*, *Luke Cage* and *Jessica Jones*, the much-lauded *Black Mirror*, *Stranger Things* and the jewel in the crown, *The Crown*. Individually, they cost anywhere from $4 million US per episode to $13 million US for *The Crown*.

It is reported that for two Jerry Seinfeld specials, plus his low-budget series, *Comedians In Cars Getting Coffee*, Netflix paid a remarkable $100 million US.

Indeed, Netflix appears to have limitless resources.

Its estimated spending on scripted shows in 2018 was
$12–$13 billion US.[17] By way of comparison, all of the
Canadian programming produced and acquired by *all* of the
Canadian conventional TV and specialty services, including
those owned by the CBC, totalled only about a quarter of
what Netflix alone spent.[18] And those dollars were spent on
shows whose budgets rarely reached $1.5 million US an hour.

Netflix is only the most visible of the big US streaming
services that has launched or will launch in Canada. Amazon
Prime, which is owned by Amazon, one of the five most valuable companies in the world, has been offering TV series for
a few years. It's estimated that it spent almost $5 billion US
on scripted shows in 2018.[19]

Bizarrely, the entry of Netflix and Amazon was eased by
the Canadian government, which neither taxed them nor
required them to contribute to the creation of Canadian
content.

The Harper government had, in fact, made it a rallying
cry that they would not tax Netflix. As we saw earlier, the
Trudeau government would pick up the Harperites' refrain
and double down, insisting that they would never tax Netflix
or — presumably — any of the other foreign broadcasting
services that might happen to enter the Canadian market.

Yet Canadian broadcasters — CTV, Global, Citytv
— have to pay tax, contribute 30 per cent of their gross
revenues to the production of Canadian shows, provide
described video and respect Canadian broadcast standards.
They have to do all this while losing money. None of the
FAANGs have to do any of these things.

The CRTC considered the hole in the garden wall again
in 2012. By then, Netflix was a rapidly expanding presence
in Canadian households, digital media advertising revenues

had almost caught up to newspapers and were taking nearly 25 per cent of the Canadian advertising market, with the majority of that slice going to Facebook and Google. For their part, the big conventional TV networks had begun to lose money for the first time in their history.

The commission concluded, however, that there was no reason to change its view on exempting digital media from regulation. The CRTC left the hole in the garden wall and extended the Digital Media Exemption Order one more time.[20]

As the commission was dithering, the Conservatives were pursuing a "consumer-friendly" agenda on behalf of "ordinary Canadians," which would end up compounding the problems of the traditional media.

In June 2012, Stephen Harper named a new chair of the CRTC, career bureaucrat Jean-Pierre Blais. He came to his position channelling the government's "consumer-friendly" agenda. Kate Taylor, the *Globe and Mail*'s culture columnist, called him "the champion of the little guy [who] positioned the CRTC as the true friend of that group the Conservative prime minister [Stephen Harper] used to call 'ordinary Canadians.'"[21]

It was a curious stance for the chairman of the commission to adopt. The *Broadcasting Act* is very clear that the job of the CRTC is to implement the objectives of the *Act*: "the Commission shall regulate and supervise all aspects of the Canadian broadcasting system . . . with a view to implementing the broadcasting policy set out in subsection 3(1) and, in so doing, shall have regard to the regulatory policy set out in subsection (2)."[22]

Neither the broadcasting policy laid out in the *Act* nor the regulatory policy make any reference to consumers. The overarching goals of the *Act* are to ensure that the system is owned and controlled by Canadians and that it produces varied Canadian programming of high quality. Nowhere does it say that the system should be regulated in the interests of Canadians as consumers. The *Act* is almost purely and completely concerned with cultural questions.

Nevertheless, almost from his first day on the job, the new chairman made clear that his mandate would be to ensure that Canadians got their broadcasting services in whatever way they wanted and at the best possible price.

There is, of course, nothing wrong with helping consumers, but it must always be done in a way that does not compromise the cultural objectives of the *Act*. This is, however, hard to do, since all the different parts of the broadcasting system are structured to support one another. Not recognizing how interdependent the pieces are can lead to calamitous results.

In the Speech from the Throne in 2013, the government pounded home its new theme, devoting a whole section of the speech to "Defending Canadian Consumers." It promised to bash the telecommunications companies on behalf of ordinary Canadians and that "Our government believes Canadian families should be able to choose the combination of television channels they want. It will require channels to be unbundled . . ."[23]

The message to the CRTC could not have been clearer.

Over the next couple of years, Netflix's growth continued, as did the growth of the FAANGs' digital advertising business.

By 2015, Netflix was in an estimated 5.3 million homes and generating over $600 million a year in revenue. Between them, Netflix and YouTube were consuming almost half of all the peak period bandwidth on computers and tablets. They were commanding more and more of Canadians' leisure time.

The consumption of Canadian TV and newspapers continued to fall, quite radically among people under fifty.

Facebook and Google were also prospering. By 2015, digital media had taken roughly 40 per cent of the Canadian advertising market. Their revenues had eclipsed those of television and were double those of newspapers. By 2016, they would be equal to those of TV and newspapers combined. The traditional Canadian media businesses fell into greater and greater difficulty.

The issue of Netflix's entry was not only about questions of relative fairness; it was also about the impact of Netflix on cable and satellite subscriptions. Its advent clearly began to have an impact on cable: Growth in the number of subscribers stalled.

When Canadians drop (or never buy) cable service, they effectively exit the Canadian broadcasting system and lose access to Canadian shows and TV news. They no longer see the Gord Downie special that nonetheless drew 11.5 million viewers, the nightly newscasts that still pull in millions every evening, *Hockey Night in Canada*, most of the great drama and comedy moments, whether it's *Rick Mercer Report*, *Murdoch Mysteries*, *Corner Gas* or *Trailer Park Boys*. When they abandon cable exclusively for Netflix, they effectively drop out of the shared national conversation.

Of course, the loss of subscribers also erodes cable's revenues. When this happens, their ability to support the financing of Canadian shows through the Canada Media Fund is compromised. This, too, has happened. Cable's contribution to the Canadian Media Fund peaked in 2015 at $254 million, and fell by 2017 to $217 million.[24]

The impact of the FAANGs on traditional media and Canadian culture was beginning to be very clear by 2015.

Given the speed with which they were growing, the new players' presence was likely to be even more corrosive in the years to come.

Against this backdrop, the CRTC organized a set of public proceedings called Let's Talk TV. They were designed to allow the new chairman, Jean-Pierre Blais, to make good on his consumer-friendly promises. In the resulting decisions, the CRTC instructed the cable companies to unbundle their packages of channels and make a pick-and-pay option available. Canadians would be able — for the first time — to take only the very popular channel and decline the narrower more specialized channels.

The cultural problem with this "consumer-friendly" approach was that it effectively killed the economics of the smaller, more niche-oriented channels. When they were no longer in the same package as the very popular channel, they did not enjoy the same level of penetration in Canadian households and, therefore, received less money from the cable companies.

The death of the smaller channels — Book TV is a good example — not only reduced the diversity of Canadian programming available, it had the perverse effect of forcing the cable companies to raise their rates for the very popular channels to maintain their margins. Thus, the bad news for ordinary Canadians was that they ended up receiving fewer channels for the same price. This, in turn, made cable look like a worse deal and encouraged further migration to Netflix.

As part of Let's Talk TV, the CRTC, once again, considered the Digital Media Exemption Order and, once again, decided to leave it intact. The commission said, "The Commission reaffirms its view that licensing digital media broadcasting undertakings is generally not necessary to achieve the broadcasting objectives set out in the *Act*. For the time being, exemptions of these services will enable continued growth and development of digital media industries in Canada."[25]

Although two Canadian competitors to Netflix had been launched in 2014 — Shomi (owned by Rogers and Shaw) and Crave (owned by Bell) — they did not stand much of a chance against Netflix. Shomi folded in 2016 and Crave struggled on. As of 2018, it had managed to attract just 1.3 million customers, about a fifth of what Netflix had.[26]

Their difficulties are not hard to understand. Netflix can lay off the costs of its expensive productions across a worldwide base of more than 120 million subscribers. It is simply impossible for Canadian competitors to match that. They can never be big enough to commission the number and quality of shows that Netflix can.

And Netflix is not the end of it. Starting to enter the Canadian market are more behemoths: CBS, Time Warner, Apple and the greatest entertainment monster of them all, Disney.

CBS All Access entered the Canadian market in May 2018 with a host of its very popular shows, including *NCIS*, the remade *Hawaii Five-0*, *Madam Secretary* and *Survivor*. Estimates are that CBS will spend more than $3 billion US on scripted shows in 2019.

Shortly after CBS launched in Canada, NBCUniversal also moved into the market. It launched Hayu, an "all-reality" streaming service that includes *Keeping Up with the Kardashians*.

This, however, is likely only the tip of the iceberg. NBCUniversal controls major TV production houses and

film studios. Its iconic franchises include the Bond, Jason
Bourne and *Fast and Furious* movies, as well as the *Law and
Order* TV series, *America's Got Talent*, *Saturday Night Live*
and *Days of Our Lives*. If and when NBCUniversal decides
fully to enter the Canadian market, it will not only have very
attractive assets, it will be backed by its owner, one of the
largest and wealthiest telecommunications companies in the
world, Comcast.

The combination of telecommunications and content
here reflects a similar strategy to that of Bell in Canada.
Comcast is betting that by using all the technical tools and
database sets available across all of its services (programming,
mobile and internet access), it will be able to establish its
brand as the place for consumers to gain the greatest benefit
in communications. What Comcast learns about consumers from its TV databases will be used to help target its sale
of internet access; what it learns about consumers from the
company's mobile databases will help target programming
offers.

The new convergence is as much about the amount of
data that can be assembled with respect to consumer behaviour as anything else. Using sophisticated analytics, the data
can be analyzed to determine consumer tastes and to target
highly specific groups with specially tailored messages. The
strategy for Comcast/NBCUniversal will be the same as
those pursued by Google and Facebook: very tight targeting
of extremely well-defined psychographic and demographic
groups.

Disney will, it is predicted, launch its streaming service
in 2019. Beyond its own shows and movies, it also owns
the Star Wars and Marvel franchises, along with Pixar, the
world's most successful animation studio. It has recently

bought 21st Century Fox's TV and film assets, which include *The Simpsons*, *Empire*, *The X-Men* franchise, *Avatar*, *Planet of the Apes* and on and on. If things go according to plan, it will be spending about $15 billion per year on films and TV series.

In entering the Canadian market, it will doubtless also leverage its theme parks — the various Disney Worlds and Disneylands — along with its merchandise. It will produce a formidable and attractive offer, anchored in one of the world's most iconic brands and featuring the most successful movies of the last ten years.

In June of 2018, AT&T received a green light from the American courts to purchase Time Warner, which owns Warner Bros. (*Harry Potter* and *Batman*), HBO (*Game of Thrones*, etc.) and CNN. The deal, like the Comcast/NBCUniversal tie up and the Bell strategy, twins a very wealthy telecommunications company with one of the world's premiere content companies. It, too, will doubtless be rolling out a major streaming service.

After the transaction concluded, the new AT&T-era boss of Time Warner, John Stankey, made clear that he wanted HBO to substantially increase "its subscriber base and the number of hours that viewers spend watching. To pull it off, the network will have to come up with more content . . . transforming itself into something bigger and broader." Inevitably this will mean the creation of many new shows and the expenditure of much more money.

In commenting on why more was essential, the new HBO head gave an excellent, succinct description of the strategy that is animating all the big, contemporary convergence plays. He said, "I want more hours of engagement. Why are more hours of engagement important? Because you get more data and information about a customer that then allows you to do things like monetise through alternate models of advertising as well as subscriptions, which is very important to play in tomorrow's world."[27]

As if Netflix, Amazon, Disney, Comcast/NBCUniversal and AT&T/Time Warner were not enough, the monsters themselves, Google and Facebook, are also entering the Canadian TV market. Google's YouTube had been here for some time with amateur videos, but has moved recently into hosting whole television channels. Facebook, too, has indicated that it will be investing in professionally produced video content. It has created revenue-sharing deals for high-end short shows and has begun buying streaming sports rights.

The resources available to Google and Facebook were practically unlimited — yet growing. By 2017, they had become, after Apple, the second- and sixth-largest companies in the world.

Google's revenues were more than $110 billion US in 2017.[28] It had a 90 per cent share of the worldwide search engine market.[29] For its part, Facebook had revenues of $41 billion US.[30] It had a 63 per cent share of the worldwide social media market.[31] Between Google and Facebook, they captured approximately 60 per cent of all the digital ad revenue in the world and 25 per cent of the advertising spend on all media.[32]

To make traditional Canadian media tremble even more, Apple, which had more cash on its balance sheet than any other company on Earth, announced in 2018 that it, too, would be entering the video content business. It has hired seasoned Hollywood executives, put aside an initial $1 billion US and signed up Oprah Winfrey. The rush into high-end

TV and movies is attracting all of the FAANGs.

The same is true of Amazon Prime. By 2017, it was spending more, much more, than all Canadian broadcasters combined.

But competition is not the only problem the unrestricted entry of these giants causes for Canadian television. They will also likely rob it of its most profitable content. For decades, CTV, Global and Citytv have made their money by buying the most popular US shows that appear on CBS, NBC, ABC and Fox and selling them to Canadian advertisers. As those companies enter the Canadian market directly, they likely will be unwilling to sell their shows to the Canadian networks. That would, of course, make the latter's already unprofitable businesses even more unattractive.

The sad truth is that the extension of the hole in the garden wall did not create room for Canadian digital broadcasters to grow. Rather, it gave carte blanche to the largest, best-heeled companies in the world. It gave the green light to Netflix and Amazon — soon to be joined by Disney/Fox, AT&T/Time Warner, Facebook, Apple and the rest — to crush their Canadian competitors while contributing nothing to Canadian culture.

As of early 2019, Netflix was the most popular television service in Canada for people under fifty-five. It consistently beat the two biggest Canadian channels, CTV and Global. It left the smaller ones, Citytv and CBC, in the dust.[33]

As if all this were not bad enough, digital pirates have emerged, stealing the signals of the major networks all over the world and either giving them away or selling them for very modest fees. It is possible to buy a box on Amazon that will provide access to thousands of TV channels for $15 a month. A study by data experts Sandvine, *Video Piracy in Canada,* estimated that close to 10 per cent of Canadian households in 2017 accessed known subscription television piracy sites (illegal services that replicate a cable or satellite service for a fraction of the cost of a legal service), representing just a portion of the full extent of video piracy.

In effect, this meant that the cable and satellite companies were short somewhere between half a million and a million subscribers that they would otherwise have. They were not, therefore, collecting $500–800 million in annual fees, with the result that they were not remitting payments to the specialty TV services of between $150 and $250 million.[34]

The combined impact of the loss of advertising revenue, the emergence of unregulated foreign broadcasters and piracy has been hugely damaging to the Canadian TV business. Between 2013 and 2017, 4,500 employees at the CBC and private television broadcast services employees were laid off — almost 25 per cent of the industry's workforce. Not surprisingly, expenditures by the big conventional channels are decreasing. They continue to lose money, while the profitability of the pay and specialty services is beginning to erode.[35]

The situation of Global was typical. Its biggest cost centre, aside from buying American shows, was its news department. It had the second-largest private TV news operation in the country, with local news shows in all the most important English cities. By 2017, it had experienced five consecutive years of increasing losses.[36] It had tried to rationalize its news business in 2018, cutting eighty positions in its bureaus across the country, while promising to hire fifty online journalists. It seemed very unlikely, however, that the digital dimes would be able to replace the lost traditional TV dollars.

Global is owned by Corus, which is controlled by the Shaw family of Calgary. The Shaws are vastly wealthy and worth roughly a billion dollars. The family controls not only the second-largest group of broadcast assets in English Canada (after Bell Media), but also the dominant cable company in Western Canada, the second-largest direct-to-home satellite service and extensive telecommunications assets.

In 2018, the Shaws clearly concluded that it was not worth hanging on to Corus, and hired investment bankers to find a buyer for their shares. Since any buyer had to be Canadian, the pool was very small. As of early 2019, the other big media companies had declined even to kick the tires. This may be because they believe that the Competition Bureau would block any deal involving them; or it may be that they agree with the Shaws and think the assets not worth having.

The papers, too, shrank dramatically. Salary and wage costs decreased by almost a third from 2012 to 2016.[37] The papers themselves have become almost unrecognizable. The big fat, multi-section behemoths are now as thin as a razor. The glory days are completely gone. All that is left are losses as far as the eye can see.

The precarious situation of Postmedia had been clear for some time. It had been losing money for many years. By 2018, it had been losing money every year but one since 2011.[38]

Paul Godfrey and GoldenTree Asset Management had bought the *National Post* and the Southam chain of newspapers in 2010, assembling all the most important broadsheets, apart from the *Globe* and the *Toronto Star*, in the most important markets in English Canada.

Godfrey was a very experienced executive and politician. Dapper and well-connected, he had had a long, successful business career. Most importantly, he knew a great deal about the newspaper industry. He had been the publisher of the *Toronto Sun* in the early 1980s and then CEO of the entire *Sun* chain. In 1996, he led a management buyout of the company and then, a couple of years later, sold it for almost a $1 billion, making himself and the other managers a good deal of money.

When Godfrey and GoldenTree bought Postmedia, they doubtless expected the financial performance of the papers to rebound with the end of the Great Recession of 2008–2009. And it did, to a certain extent. Where the chain had a before-tax loss of over $130 million in 2009, it posted a small profit in 2010.

The problem was, however, that the return to profitability was based on cost-cutting and not on improvements in revenue. Indeed, starting in 2010, both advertising and subscription revenue began a steady and ever steeper decline.

Between 2009 and 2018, advertising revenue fell by almost 60 per cent, from $740 million a year to $308 million. Through this period, the company laboured mightily to strengthen their digital presence. They rebuilt their papers for all platforms, made partnerships with companies like Mogo Financial Technology and significantly strengthened their ability to combine digital ads with search and social media. While digital revenue grew, it only increased by $37 million over the period, not nearly enough to make up the shortfall.

As the company's revenues shrank, its executives undertook extensive restructuring. Between 2009 and 2015, total operating costs were reduced by a third. But no matter how quickly they cut, revenues fell faster, bleeding away to Google and Facebook.

In 2016, Godfrey managed to get his debt holders to agree to a significant haircut. It dropped the annual interest payments from over $72 million a year to less than $33 million. But still, it was not enough.

In a search for synergies, Postmedia bought the *Sun* chain in 2016. With this acquisition, Postmedia became the largest newspaper group in the country, controlling almost all the local dailies outside of Toronto. Yet the Competition Bureau did not block the takeover. It ruled instead that the precarious financial situation of the industry warranted allowing it to go forward.

After the operations were combined, management looked for further cost savings, while trying to maintain the combined revenues. Between 2016 and 2018, over $175 million in costs were taken out of the newly merged chain. But still, it was not enough.

Although Postmedia made a tiny before-tax profit in 2017, the continuing relentless erosion of its advertising revenue drove it back into losses in 2018. The boat was taking on so much water that it was proving impossible to bail fast enough to keep it afloat. The clear and present danger was that its investors and bankers would run out of patience before it was able make the much sought after "digital transition."

Postmedia's closure would mean that there would no longer be any local papers in many of Canada's biggest cities. The *Vancouver Sun* and *Province*, the *Calgary Sun* and *Herald*, the *Edmonton Sun* and *Journal*, the *Ottawa Citizen* and *Sun*, the *Windsor Star*, the *Montreal Gazette*, the *Regina Leader-Post*, the *Saskatoon StarPhoenix* and many, many smaller ones would go down.

Some of these papers are among the oldest in the country. The *Gazette* was founded in 1778, the *Ottawa Citizen* in 1845, the *Vancouver Sun* in 1912, the *Regina Leader-Post* in 1883. In some cases, in other words, they predated the country. In almost all cases, they are the oldest links to their cities' cultural past.

The experience of Postmedia illustrates very clearly how profoundly the structural transformation of communications has affected traditional media. Godfrey and his management team did all the classically correct things to save their empire. They cut costs relentlessly, gave their debt holders a giant haircut, made a merger to find synergies and further cost savings and aggressively expanded their digital offer. Still, none of it has been enough.

The most important piece of the remaining business, aside from the *Globe and Mail*, is Torstar. It owns a raft of newspapers, including — among others — the *Toronto Star*, the *Hamilton Spectator*, the *Peterborough Examiner* and the Metroland Group, which comprises more than a hundred community newspapers. The company had been started in 1892, just twenty-five years after Confederation.

Like Postmedia, the Torstar group had been aggressively pursuing a digital strategy. It, too, had made its papers available on all platforms, expanded into other digital services and dramatically increased its analytic capabilities both to improve its content and to assist advertisers more effectively.

Seeing that Postmedia was struggling, Torstar daringly launched an expansion in April 2018, transforming the Metro papers that it owned in Halifax, Calgary, Vancouver and Edmonton. It rebranded them *StarMetro Halifax*, *StarMetro Calgary*, etc. and promised to expand their local coverage in all those cities.

At the beginning of 2019, it was not at all clear that the expansion would succeed and halt the revenue decline.

Torstar had been posting losses before tax since 2013.[39] Given the structural problems confronting the industry, the expansion may only make the situation worse. The company's most recent financials were not promising. For the first three quarters of 2018 compared to the first three quarters for 2017, revenues were down by $48 million (-10.7 per cent). Operating losses had been reduced from $32 million to $20 million by reducing costs by $50 million, including a $26 million reduction in compensation costs.[40] The danger arose that for Torstar — like Postmedia — they may run out of cash before they can complete the "digital transition."

The efforts of Postmedia, Torstar and their Canadian news companies to expand their digital offers have so far enjoyed very limited success. The most popular websites in Canada are overwhelmingly American. This is true in general, and for news. In 2015, only seven of the top twenty news sites were Canadian.[41]

It all adds up to a bleak picture. If the newspapers and conventional TV news collapse, the industry will be down to one, the CBC. Apart from that source, Canadians will then be reduced to getting their news from foreign news sources, almost all of which will be American.

Curiously, the only part of the digital world that has been going well for Canadians is pornography. The biggest collection of pornographic websites in the world is owned by MindGeek, a Montreal-based company. They own Pornhub, YouPorn, RedTube and a host of others. They are a sort of YouTube for porn. They claim over 100 million viewers a day. According to David Auerbach in *Slate*, MindGeek's pornography empire consumes more bandwidth than Facebook or Amazon. On listings of the top websites in North America, the company ranks eighth, below Google, Facebook, YouTube and Yahoo, but ahead of Reddit, Twitter and Instagram. This is an impressive achievement. It is reassuring to know that there is at least one Canadian cultural success in the online world.

CHAPTER 6

The Sleepy Gardeners: The Justin Trudeau Years

The victory of the Liberals in 2015 was accomplished, in part, through the use of highly targeted advertising on the big US social media platforms. The Liberals had learned a great deal from Obama's success in the US and were proud of the modernity of their efforts.

In 2012, the Obama campaign had created one of the largest and most sophisticated voter databases ever assembled. They had merged VoteBuilder, the Democrats' file of 190 million voters with the party's list of 23 million supporters on Facebook. This allowed the campaign to target the "influencers" in very specific demographics with messages tailored precisely for them, ensuring that the right messages went to the right people. It also strengthened the targeting by having the influencers share it with their friends and colleagues. Shared messaging is not only cheaper than mass mailings, it is also more effective. People are more likely to believe something sent to them by someone they trust.

Taking a leaf from the Obama playbook, the Liberals used social media very actively during the 2015 election, outspending the Tories and focusing their efforts on young people who — as their chief digital strategist, Tom Pitfield, put it — "really do share content." He contrasted the Liberal approach with that of the Conservatives, saying: "I think the Conservatives focussed on . . . the old way of doing campaigns," conducting focus groups to find messages that would "resonate" and then "carpet bombing" the airwaves and telephone lines.

"The problem with the traditional approach is that 25 per cent of Canadians now have only cellphones and 42 per cent of them don't watch television. So, if you're not digital, you're pretty much marginalising a quarter to a third of your vote."[1]

This approach to communicating with Canadians continued once the Liberals took power. Between November 2015 and May 2017, the Liberal government spent almost $14 million on social media advertising.[2] For anyone on the new digital platforms, Justin Trudeau was omnipresent, enjoying over 6 million followers on Facebook, more than 2 million on Instagram and 4 million on Twitter.

Like Obama, the Liberals took a very positive view of the big Silicon Valley companies. They saw them not only as the vanguard of the new economy, but — like the Liberals themselves — progressive and liberal on all manner of subjects.

The prime minister was avowedly feminist and technologically innovative. He led the party of "now." Asked why half his cabinet were women, Trudeau replied, "because it's 2015." The remark might have applied equally well to his attitude toward big tech. As Sean Silcoff put it in the *Globe and Mail*, "Prime Minister Trudeau has fashioned himself as a progressive champion of the 21st-century ideas economy built on the 'resourcefulness' of Canadians. To accomplish that, his government has committed to fund venture capitalists, artificial intelligence institutes, female entrepreneurs and clean tech initiatives . . ."[3]

The early Trudeau government tied itself both in image terms and substantively to the cool, progressive tech wizards at the FAANGs.

The prime minister was seen at Davos in the company of Sheryl Sandberg, the chief operating officer of Facebook He went to San Francisco, the first prime minister to do so since 1945, to visit Silicon Valley and meet with the tech lords. In Toronto, he could be seen talking and hanging out with the executives of Google and Facebook. He was happy to be on hand for announcements about Google's takeover of a portion of the Toronto waterfront through its affiliate Sidewalk Labs.[4]

The FAANGs were well-received by the prime minister and his office in Ottawa. As of 2018, Google lobbyists had met with the prime minister at least five times and with members of his office staff separately another ten. They had, as well, blanketed much of the rest of the government, meeting with senior officials, MPs, political staff and ministers from finance, foreign affairs, international trade, infrastructure and communities and innovation, science and economic development. Between August 2016 and early 2019, Google had more than sixty meetings to lobby the government.

Trudeau's first minister of Canadian heritage, Mélanie Joly, was — if anything — even keener to prove her digital bona fides. She was, as she liked to say, a "digital native" and liked to be surrounded by other digital natives.

Not to be outdone by the prime minister, her first chief of staff was from Google. Joly, like the PM, met with Google lobbyists personally on at least five different occasions, and her chief of staff six times in the first six months of 2017. They were apparently discussing broadcasting policy.

Joly liked to be seen in the company of FAANG folk and went to Silicon Valley on at least three different occasions. In April 2017 she met with each of the FAANGs.[5] Later that same year, she went back and met with YouTube, Facebook, Twitter and Google. She went once more at the beginning of 2018 to meet with the FAANGs and to deliver a speech at the acme of Silicon Valley, Stanford University.[6]

So entangled was Joly with Google that questions began to be asked in the House of Commons about potential conflicts of interest.

Google's meetings with top government officials were paralleled by Netflix. It met extensively with Joly's chief of staff at the Department of Heritage, as well as her other most senior officials. The *Citizen* reported that between January 2017 and May 2018 Netflix met twenty-three times with all manner of important government types, including people in the Prime Minister's Office.[7]

The peculiar thing about all these visits and meetings is that nothing seemed to come of them. Talks took place, position papers were doubtless given out, and many coffees consumed, but nothing happened. With the exception of Joly's ill-fated Netflix deal, discussed in Chapter 1, nobody said anything about the conduct of the FAANGs, let alone what the government should do about them. There was no mention of their impact on the advertising markets, their effect on Canadian media or the social and cultural problems that followed in their wake.

To the contrary, the Liberals continued to embrace the FAANGs, saluting their small gestures of largesse and letting them operate in Canada untouched by Canadian tax law or regulations. As noted earlier, they even adopted the Harper government's rallying cry that they would not tax

Netflix. When asked why, they rehashed the prime minister's undertaking not to tax the middle class, which made no sense, since they had junked all sorts of more important campaign promises. It was hard to understand their reasoning. Perhaps it was meant to symbolise their commitment to the high-tech future. Who, after all, would want to hinder its coming?

Yet the enthusiastic embrace of the FAANGs represented a very different positioning from what was going on in the rest of the world. Throughout Europe, and in Japan, Australia and the United States, governments were starting to treat the FAANGs with great suspicion. The Europeans had been looking into their conduct as early as 2010. Over the next few years, they took exception to the FAANGs' failure to protect individual privacy, their propensity to distribute fake news, bullying and hate speech, their intensely anti-competitive conduct and their negative impact on local domestic cultures.

While anti-trust issues may seem a little remote from matters of cultural policy, it is worth spending a moment on them. They serve to illustrate just how rapacious the FAANGs had become. And the way they'd been pursued by other governments shows not only how broad their concerns were, but also underlines how profoundly passive the Canadian government has been. It is not just that the government had failed to move on tax issues or Netflix's failure to contribute to the making of Canadian TV; it had not moved on any front. It had stood by and watched as one calamity after another had shaken the Western democracies, its hands folded, seeing no evil. The contrast with how other governments dealt with the FAANGs could not be more stark.

Throughout all the advanced economies, special studies were undertaken, parliamentary committees formed and enquiries established to decide how best to deal with the negative consequences of the FAANGS' presence and behaviour. In many jurisdictions, the offices of the giants were raided and they were charged with specific offences. European courts and tribunals imposed colossal fines for everything from lying to illegally destroying competitors and distributing fake news.

The Canadian government's decision not to tax Netflix (or any other foreign digital services), while continuing to tax their Canadian competitors, was not the policy followed anywhere else. "Along with the European Union, New Zealand, Australia, Norway, South Korea, Japan, Switzerland and South Africa [had all] introduced measures to begin collecting GST or HST equivalents (VAT) on digital online services."[8]

Indeed, the Europeans went much farther. They were increasingly concerned that the FAANGs were not only not paying sales tax, but were actively engaged in tax avoidance. The most infamous case was Apple's use of Ireland as a tax haven, allowing the company to avoid paying tax anywhere outside of the United States.

Just four years after Apple was created, it established an Irish holding company through which it flowed its foreign earnings. The arrangements that the company struck with the Irish government allowed Apple "to pay no tax to any government . . . [and] claim tax residence nowhere." This manoeuvre was not engineered because Apple was poor. It had over $230 billion US in cash and investments, the largest cash hoard of any company in the world.[9]

The Europeans took a dim view of this arrangement and

levied a roughly $15 billion US fine. That this was a tiny portion of Apple's cash on hand demonstrates what the tax expert Lee Sheppard calls "Silicon Valley's well-known vanity and contempt for government . . ."[10] It demonstrates the company's greed and unwillingness to be a good corporate citizen in the countries where it made its money.

Tax-avoidance engineering was not restricted to Apple. The European authorities were also concerned about the other FAANGs. According to estimates by the Organisation for Economic Cooperation and Development, "such strategies cost governments around the world as much as $240 billion (US) a year in lost revenue," according to a 2015 estimate. As a result, the treasuries of those countries were disadvantaged, as were the companies competing with the FAANGs in their home markets.[11]

Taxation problems were only the tip of the iceberg for the Europeans. They were equally concerned about the anti-competitive conduct of the FAANGs, particularly the behaviour of Google and Facebook. Estimates vary, but Google appeared to control more than 90 per cent of the search market in Europe. It was also dominant in digital advertising, taking as much as 60 per cent of all revenue. In effect, Google enjoyed a virtual monopoly.[12]

Google was, as a result, so rich and powerful that it could either buy its rivals or crush them.

The European competition authorities began investigating various aspects of Google's behaviour in 2010. In 2017, the European Commission levied a $2.7 billion US fine for illegal behaviour. This was more than double the previous largest fine ever imposed.[13]

The basis for the fine was that Google had advantaged its own services when search results were shown. "The antitrust decision related to Google's online shopping service, which the European Commission . . . said had received preferential treatment compared with those of rivals in specialized search results, . . . such so-called "vertical" search products — also include those for restaurants and business reviews — represent a fast-growing percentage of Google's annual revenues."[14]

The European competition authorities also looked into Google's use of Android to cement its dominance in search and browsing. They found that in striking deals with Smartphone manufacturers, Google imposed agreements that "required Google's services, such as its search bar and Chrome browser, to be favoured over rival offerings." Google had used Android as a vehicle to establish the dominance of its search engine. A fine of $5.1 billion US was imposed, the largest fine ever levied.[15]

Similar concerns about Google's conduct also emerged in the United States, where Google had been accused of disadvantaging various "vertical" search engines. It did this, according to its critics, by "programming its search engine to ignore other sites doing the same thing that Google was doing, . . . making it nearly impossible for competing vertical search engines to show up high in Google's results."[16]

A number of websites complained about Google's conduct to the US Federal Trade Commission. Yelp, TripAdvisor, Citysearch and Getty Images all described abusive conduct on Google's part, from raising their prices by 10,000 per cent to threatening to kick them off the website altogether. Getty's general counsel described Google's response to their complaints: "'Well, if you don't agree to these terms,' Google said, 'we'll just exclude you' . . . [which is] not really a choice, because if you aren't on Google, you basically don't exist."[17]

Google's use of Android also came under scrutiny in the US, as it had in Europe. There was, for example, Skyhook Wireless, "which had invented a new navigation system that competed with Google's location software and had signed major deals with cell phone manufacturers Samsung and Motorola (both of which use the Android platform). A high-ranking Google official pressured Samsung and Motorola to end the relationship with Skyhook — and implied that if they didn't, Google would make it impossible for them to ship their phones on time . . . Soon, Samsung and Motorola cancelled their Skyhook contracts."[18]

As early as 2012, Federal Trade Commission staff had written a 160-page memo that said "Google had adopted a strategy of demoting, or refusing to display, links to certain vertical websites in highly commercial categories . . . Google's conduct has resulted — and will result — in real harm to consumers and innovation."[19]

It was not just Google's conduct that worried competition regulators. Facebook, too, had been the subject of close examination by the Europeans. When Facebook bought WhatsApp, it claimed that it could not link the WhatsApp and Facebook user profiles and would not do so, even if it could. The acquisition was approved on the basis that data would not be shared between the two platforms.

Three months after the approvals were granted, Facebook did exactly what it said that it couldn't and wouldn't do: It linked the user profiles. Needless to say, the European regulators weren't pleased to have been misled. In May 2017 they fined Facebook 110 million euros.[20] France and Germany then followed suit and ordered Facebook to stop sharing data.

Beyond these issues, the Europeans became increasingly concerned that the FAANGs had become malign influences on their social and cultural life. They were worried about the companies' tendency to breach users' privacy, erode local cultures and provide platforms for the dissemination of abusive and threatening conduct, fake news and hate speech.

Of all these issues, the most troubling were the problems of fake news, trolling and hate speech. Their intersection could be seen most clearly in the revelations about Cambridge Analytica, where the Facebook profiles of some 87 million people were "improperly harvested." They were then used to create detailed psychographic profiles that were targeted during the American election to help elect Donald Trump, and, in the UK, to assist the Leave forces during the referendum on membership in the European Union. According to Chris Wylie, the Canadian whistleblower who was involved in the work, "the company took fake news to the next level."[21]

The Cambridge Analytica scandal rolled together many of the concerns that had been expressed about the increasingly corrosive influence Facebook and Google were having on social and political life. The platforms — particularly Facebook — had been weaponized through big data mining to influence the outcome of elections by promoting hate speech, social division and fake news.

For Mark Zuckerberg, the CEO of Facebook, the Cambridge Analytica scandal had morphed into an enormous problem. He was called to testify before the American Congress and various of his senior executives to the House of Commons in London and the European parliament. In March 2018, the Federal Trade Commission opened a new investigation into Facebook's privacy practices. The Securities and Exchange Commission also started an inquiry, as had the Federal Bureau of Investigation.

In the UK, the raids on Cambridge Analytica were followed with Facebook being hit with the largest fine the Information Commissioner's Office could levy. It went on to note that "it was pursuing a criminal prosecution of SCL Elections, the company from which Cambridge Analytica was spun out . . . Another company linked to Cambridge Analytica, AggregateIQ, also faces punishment for its involvement."[22]

For its part, the UK parliament's Digital, Culture, Media and Sport Committee released a wide-ranging, damning report on fake news, the use of data and "dark" ads in elections. The report offered a "wide ranging critique that carried with it the full weight of parliament."[23] It "sets out in great detail what is known about fake news, data targeting, Cambridge Analytica, Facebook and Russian interference, and issues a set of demands that include new regulations, legislation, codes of ethics and police investigations. It calls for 'algorithmic' auditing, for the heavily guarded secrets of the tech companies' 'black boxes' to be smashed open, for a digital version of Ofcom [the CRTC of the UK] to be established and for companies to be held legally liable for harmful or illegal content." The select committee was particularly scathing in its discussion of Facebook's participation in its proceedings, accusing it of obfuscating, failing to investigate and outright lying.

The British government said that new legislation would be brought forward in late 2018 to deal with the problems identified by the committee.

This problem of fake news had only added to the long list of concerns that had been raised in the last few years. These have included online bullying so vicious that it resulted in suicides. Amanda Todd, a Canadian Grade 10 student, was so aggressively attacked by a man in Holland that she hanged herself. A year later, Rehtaeh Parsons, then fifteen, was gang raped by four boys who posted the rape online. The resulting humiliation and further bullying caused her, too, to take her life.

The problem of online bullying is not unique to Canada. It appears to be happening wherever social media are present. In the UK, for example, a recent study found that half of young people have "experienced threatening, intimidating or abusive messages on social media, pushing some to the verge of suicide in the most extreme cases."[24] In response, the UK government was developing an internet safety strategy that would involve the creation of a bullying prevention hub.[25]

The problem of cyber bullying is closely related to the dissemination of hate speech and the fabrication of fake news. This came to light most graphically in North America when it became clear that trolls paid for by the Russian government had attempted to influence the outcome of the 2016 US election in favour of Donald Trump. They made up fake news stories that were designed either to deceive Americans about the positions of the two major parties or to sow dissent.

The operation of fake news is particularly insidious. It has its own dynamic. Because there is a natural human tendency to be most interested in stories that are out of the ordinary or that involve strong emotions, there is a built-in bias within social media to emphasize them. The algorithms direct people to the most-viewed posts. And as the most-viewed posts are often the most extreme, the machine dishes them up with greater frequency.

The more extreme and unlikely the information is, the more it also leads people to look more deeply into it. A recent study at MIT described the effect this way: "What we are witnessing is the computational exploitation of a natural human desire to 'look behind the curtain,' to dig deeper into something that engages us. As we click and click, we are carried along by the exciting sensation of uncovering more secrets and deeper truths. YouTube leads viewers down a rabbit hole of extremism, while Google (its parent) racks up the ad sales."[26]

These effects mean that fake news and hoaxes are more likely to be viewed and more likely to be shared. A study in *Science* showed that fake news stories spread faster than real ones.

Social media make money by keeping people on a site as long as possible. That way, they are exposed to the maximum number of ads. This creates a bias toward the most dangerous and offensive materials. "Designed to maximise user time on site, it [Facebook] promotes whatever wins the most attention. Posts that tap into negative, primal emotions like anger or fear, studies have found, produce the highest engagement and so proliferate."[27] These effects can become most intense during times of extreme partisanship and stress. By the end of the 2016 election in the United States, "the top fake stories were generating more engagement than the top real ones."

To make matters worse, the costs of distributing fake news are very small. The Russian trolls spent an estimated $100,000 US to reach 126 million Americans during the campaign that elected Donald Trump.[28]

As fake news and hate speech came to be increasingly available on social media, people around the world reduced their consumption of true news. They were disconnecting from traditional news outlets — whether newspapers or TV — and relying more and more on social media. For roughly 40 per cent of Canadians, Facebook was their primary source of news.[29]

Moves began in the American Congress to deal with the problem of fake news. The Mueller probe indicted a number of the Russians involved in trolling the US election, while in the US Senate various bills were prepared addressing the topic. The one that appeared most advanced as of late 2018 was the *Honest Ads Act*, which was introduced by Senator Mark Warner, a legislator with a very strong background in technology.[30]

The problem of hate speech had preoccupied the Europeans for some time. Not surprisingly, perhaps, Germany was particularly sensitive. When it became clear that Facebook had started to be used by neo-Nazi groups to promote hatred and Holocaust denial, the government became so alarmed that it passed legislation threatening Facebook with 50-million-euro-a-day fines if it did not take down such materials within twenty-four hours.

While the Europeans were tackling the problems of hate speech, bullying and fake news, they did not lose sight of the cultural implications of the FAANGs' activities. They were particularly focussed on the tidal wave of new and foreign audio-visual materials that had washed into their smart-phones and computers.

In May 2018, the European Union announced an agreement to amend its audio-visual rules. In the words of the Parliament, "the new law extends European broadcast rules to online video services."

The centrepiece of the new policy was a requirement that Netflix and Amazon devote at least 30 per cent of their on-demand catalogue to European content. If the rules had been in place in 2018, twenty-seven of the eighty-two films that Netflix commissioned would have been European. To put that in perspective, Warner Bros.' 2018 slate, the biggest in Hollywood, was only twenty-three movies. Similarly, of the 100 new scripted shows, thirty would have to be European.[31]

The new rules required, as well, that Netflix and Amazon could not meet the 30 per cent target by simply buying shows that had already been made. They would have to fund new movies and TV series. The amount that they would have to spend would be based on the proportion of the companies' revenues a particular country represented.

The 30 per cent rule extended beyond traditional audio-visual content to the user-generated materials on Facebook and YouTube. Any platform, in fact, that had any kind of audio-visual content would have to ensure that it met the 30 per cent standard.[32]

The new rules also dealt with what has historically been known as "broadcast standards," which are more or less the same in all the great democracies. They require that news appearing on broadcasters' networks be accurate and reliable. They require, as well, that their programming cannot be abusive or discriminate against groups based on race, ethnicity, sex, age or sexual orientation.[33]

In the case of the new European rules, they required that "video sharing platforms will have to take measures against content 'inciting violence, hatred and terrorism.' They need, as well, to provide 'transparent' mechanisms for users to report such content."[34] The rules covered not only Instagram, YouTube, Facebook, Google, et al., but also all real-time streaming platforms, like Periscope.

More broadly, across Europe and the US, politicians and

regulators had been moving for a number of years to deal with the bad behaviour of the FAANGs. By 2018, the pace of their efforts was, if anything, accelerating. Commissions of inquiry, police raids, parliamentary hearings were growing like mushrooms all over the Western world.

The image of the FAANGs was also changing dramatically. Where once they had been seen as models of technological sophistication and progressive values, they were increasingly viewed as a menace to the traditional supports of the liberal order. The dream of an open internet where everyone was their own publisher in an era of unparalleled freedom of expression had morphed into something that more and more resembled its opposite.

Since at least 2016, there had been a growing "techlash." The FAANGs were seen as too big, too predatory, too irresponsible and too American. There were increasing calls for them to be restructured, or — at the very least — to be treated like public utilities and regulated. Economists in the United States and Europe were beginning to propose that, as with the old monopolies of Standard Oil, AT&T and Microsoft, the best thing would be to break them up.

Whatever the outcome of these discussions, the attitude toward the FAANGs had changed profoundly. They were no longer seen as harbingers of a bright new future but as a threat to the conduct of civilized discourse and contributors to the overall coarsening of public life.

While the rest of the world was struggling to come to grips with the emergence of the FAANGs, there was a strange silence in the Peaceable Kingdom.

The minister of finance reiterated in late 2017 that the government would not be applying HST to Netflix. He then fell into a deep silence on next steps for digital services generally. He gave no indication — unlike his counterparts in the rest of the industrialized world — that he would be moving to impose sales tax on any of the digital platforms.

He was silent, as well, on the payment of corporate taxes by the FAANGs. No studies on the issue were forthcoming from finance, let alone a move like the European Union's to ensure that the giants were paying their fair share in Canada. All was silence and tranquility.

The Competition Bureau, too, was very quiet. Despite the giant fines imposed in Europe on Google and Facebook, the work of the Federal Trade Commission in the US, and the other reviews that were taking place throughout the world, no actions were initiated. The bureau looked at Google but concluded, unlike its European counterparts, that there was nothing untoward about its behaviour. Instead, the bureau's boldest moves came in the areas of bread pricing, when it claimed that Canada's largest bakeries had colluded to fix prices. It also moved on the foundering newspaper industry, raiding Torstar and Postmedia's offices at the end of 2017 and continuing their investigations through 2018.

On the fake news front, the government's slumbers were briefly interrupted by the Cambridge Analytica scandal. A parliamentary committee heard from Chris Wylie, who testified that a firm from Victoria called AggregateIQ had been tangled up with Cambridge Analytica. He said that they were involved in "money laundering" and that their senior officials "completely disregarded the concept of truth."

AggregateIQ's CEO, Zack Massingham, appeared to rebut the charges. His appearance was not a success. The committee members felt that his testimony had been "totally false" and full of "complete fabrications." They considered contempt charges against him.

Massingham infuriated the committee further by declining to show up a second time. He sent his chief operating officer instead, who was accused by Liberal MP Frank Baylis "of aiding and abetting crimes by creating tools for data harvesting and spoofing caller IDs."[35]

The committee's attacks on AggregateIQ went on for some time, with members expressing various degrees of outrage and distress. Finally, rather than investigating the matter thoroughly and producing a report, as the UK government had done, the Liberals swept the whole matter under the carpet. They referred the issue to the Privacy Commissioner, asking only that he look at the very narrow question of whether any personal information of Canadians had been compromised in the Cambridge Analytica/Facebook breach. The associated issues of data targeting, trolling and the erosion of democracy were left to one side.

When it came to the problem of fake news, however, the government attempted to strike a more activist tone. It was hard not to, since it had been a subject of unrelenting public discussion following the American election in 2016.

The prime minister admonished Sheryl Sandberg, the chief operating officer of Facebook, when he met her in Davos in 2017. He warned her that unless Facebook did something to stem the flow of fake news, it would be regulated.

When asked by journalists about the problem, he said, "That's something that I've actively asked our minister of democratic institutions to lean in on and develop tools to protect Canadians and our electoral process."[36]

For her part, said minister, Karina Gould, seemed stumped by the request. She did not propose any new "tools"; rather she said that she hoped Facebook would fix things, but lamented the fact that "the companies have so far been reluctant to take responsibility."

At the same time, she noted that "social media companies only respond when regulations come down from government." But rather than making regulations, she reassured the Canadian public by noting that she was watching what was happening in Europe.

For its part, Facebook reportedly said that federal government officials "had not made any specific requests of it." Rather, it was reported that at a meeting with Facebook in 2017, "Canadian government officials made it clear that their top priority was to convince the company to build a data centre in Canada."[37]

Apart from occasional hand-wringing, the government had, as of early 2019, made no moves to deal with the fake news issue. This was particularly surprising because topmost members of the Liberal administration were being targeted. False stories circulated on social media that Gerald Butts, the prime minister's principal secretary, "amassed a fortune of U.S. $23 million while working for the Ontario and Canadian governments." In another case, a false account purporting to represent Environment Minister Catherine McKenna claimed she was "against politicians paying for their own lunches."[38]

The approach of the government seemed always to be that it was Facebook's problem to solve. Very occasionally, it talked in vague generalities about regulating social media, but no draft regulations emerged.

When it came to cultural matters, the approach seemed to be more or less the same. Putting aside the disastrous Netflix deal, which the minister of heritage increasingly described as "transitional," she spent a good deal of time talking about the "responsibilities" of the FAANGs. She claimed that "the fundamental problem is that the FAANGs don't recognise their responsibilities . . . They need to make a fundamental change in their cultures."[39]

In a speech in early 2018 at Stanford, Minister Joly described fairly clearly the cultural challenge posed by the FAANGs. She pointed to their impact on "our democratic institutions, national security and the future of journalism." She grouched about the filter bubbles that increasingly polarize public discussion, the algorithmic bias of their discovery engines and the negative effects on artists. She concluded that the FAANGs need "to respect our cultural policies and better share the benefits linked to their business model."[40]

The same general line was pursued by the prime minister. His spokesman, Cameron Ahmad, fulminated that "the amount of fake and misleading information and accounts targeting elected officials and diminishing the debate on social media platforms . . . is increasingly concerning and frankly unacceptable." He added, "social media companies should immediately take action to fight back against those who deceive and manipulate for political gain."[41]

The landscape in Ottawa as of early 2019 was thoroughly denuded on all the manifold issues raised by the FAANGs. Nowhere had the government recognized that its job is to tax fairly, ensure markets operate properly, close down hate speech, protect Canadian culture or stop the distribution of fake news. In all its statements it appeared as a supplicant, asking the Facebooks and Googles, please, to behave better.

The government also seemed not to have seen how these issues were being dealt with in the rest of the world. It should have been emboldened by the fact that Europe had addressed many of the problems and that the FAANGs, with some grumbling, had accepted the new regulations on privacy, hate and culture. Ottawa needed only to cite and use the European precedents to be able to move forward. But it did not.

It was as though Canada existed in a world hermetically sealed from the outside. There was nothing to learn from others. In its report to Mélanie Joly, *Harnessing Change: The Future of Programming Distribution in Canada*, the CRTC provided only one footnote. It said, "Many nations around the world have similar concerns and are considering best approaches to ensure that global online services meet social responsibilities in a way that are similar to domestic industries (for example, the new and revised content requirements being considered by the European Union)."[42]

This — a footnote of acknowledgement in a report — stands as a good representation of the government's engagement. It's about as far as one could get from deFAANGing.

In smaller matters of cultural policy, the government seemed to be gripped by the same torpor.

Many commentators had suggested that it was imperative to reform the Canadian Periodical Fund. The difficulty was that the fund's machinery was all analog. To determine whether a magazine was in conformity with the fund's regulations and how much money it should receive, bureaucrats were obliged to use rulers to measure how much Canadian content is on each page.

For the magazine owners, however, the important thing was to go digital. They must do so both to save costs and to serve their customers, most of whom wanted their subscriptions online. But digital magazines did not qualify for the subsidy. This created a terrible dilemma: either abandon the future or abandon the subsidy.

The magazine owners and their trade association pressed the Department of Canadian Heritage to take the necessary steps to move the fund into the digital age. After five years of discussions, nothing had happened. It is perhaps not surprising, therefore, that Rogers Media threw in the towel in 2018 and put Canada's largest collection of magazines on the block, including *Maclean's*, *Chatelaine* and *Canadian Business*.

In a similar vein, the FairPlay coalition made a carefully thought out proposal to put an end to piracy in 2018. The coalition consisted of pretty much everyone in the TV and movie businesses: theatre owners, actors, producers, directors, record producers, Bell, Rogers, the CBC and on and on.

The coalition asked the CRTC to allow the internet service providers to block any website that was making stolen films and TV shows available. The CRTC declined on the grounds that it did not have the power in law to do so. When the FairPlay coalition then turned to the government for relief, it was fobbed off to a parliamentary committee. There was no sense on the part of the government that hundreds of millions of dollars draining out of the Canadian cultural ecosystem was an urgent problem.

It was hard to understand the terrible inertia that had gripped the government on cultural policy. Whether on small issues like fixing the Periodical Fund or larger ones like dealing with the FAANGs, the Liberal government seemed seized by a tremendous exhaustion. It made Rip Van Winkle look like the Energizer Bunny.

CHAPTER 7

The Manifesto

The hour is very late.

If the federal government does not wake from its torpor, the major Canadian media companies are likely to collapse and bring down the film and television production industries with them. If this happens, English Canada will be effectively culturally annexed by the United States.

The question is whether anything can be done to restore the garden, to root out the dog-strangling vine and the Japanese knotweed. Can the garden be untangled?

Some key principles apply in answering this question.

First, content is king. Canadian content is what matters culturally. The key thing is to ensure the production and distribution of Canadian content: Canadian books, films, news, TV shows, YouTube videos and magazines.

Ways of distributing content come and go. Once it was strictly paper, then radio waves and now digital networks. Building the garden is a perpetual project that addresses the distribution technologies of each period to ensure that Canadian content is made and can be easily accessed by Canadians. Every cultural policy, regulation, subsidy or tax arrangement must contribute to strengthening Canadian content. All the rest is housekeeping.

The second principle is that nobody can predict what is to come. The pace of change is rapid. So, whatever arrangements are put in place, they must not foreclose the future. They must, in fact, be designed to allow Canadian media and culture to evolve as technology, audience tastes and markets change.

This means that policy needs to be agnostic with respect to which kinds of content will matter, which platforms will prevail and which producers will succeed. Policy needs to allow the future of Canadian content to unfold naturally, without trying to pick winners.

It needs to allow Canadian culture to develop not — as the Great One might say — where the puck is, but where it is going. Attempting to second-guess the future is a recipe for irrelevance.

Third, the new policy must strengthen Canadian democracy and trust among its citizens. Content that encourages hatred and intolerance and content that traffics in falsehoods erode the bonds that bind us to our most basic freedoms. Everyone who produces and distributes content must be responsible for its accuracy and truthfulness. The standards that currently prevail for newspapers and broadcasters must be met by all.

What would a new cultural policy that respected these principles look like?

The first question to be answered is what does it mean for Canadian content to be king? What is it that is king?

The current definition of Canadian content, whether for television or film is, as described in Chapter 2, whatever is made by a Canadian company employing Canadians in the creative team.

Canadian content is thus whatever Canadians make. This is a weirdly industrial and employment-based definition of

"Canadian." It makes no reference to the actual content. It allows films and TV shows to be subsidized with taxpayer dollars even if they have nothing whatever to do with Canada.

A good example of what can happen is *Flashpoint*. It was made for CBS and CTV. It was a very successful, beautifully made, critically admired, prize winning, all-Canadian show: the producer, show runners, directors and lead actors were all Canadian. The show was very popular, too.

It was ostensibly set in Toronto, but when you looked at it, it was hard to see anything Canadian. The police uniforms just said "police." The arm patches did not say Toronto police; nor were there the crowns and maple leaves associated with the different ranks of the Toronto police. The story lines were fairly generic, things that might happen anywhere, but often felt ripped from US headlines. There were episodes involving white supremacists, Mexican drug gangs and bank foreclosures on houses at the high point of the US mortgage crisis. The show certainly did not feel boldly and unapologetically Canadian. What is the point of spending taxpayers' money on shows that won't even say that they are us, let alone stories that seem to reflect the preoccupations of another country?

This is not an isolated example. There has always been a problem with Canadian producers trying to disguise Canadian shows as American. Toronto turns into Chicago; Vancouver becomes Seattle. The producers do this to sell the shows in the US. And indeed the US market requires — because Americans are generally quite parochial — that the shows be about Americans and be set in the United States.

It is often difficult for a producer to resist the Americanization of a movie or a TV show. The US market is vast compared to English Canada; American broadcasters and distributors can, therefore, pay much more for a show than any Canadian could or would. Put bluntly, an American sale is almost always much more valuable to a Canadian producer than anything that could be realized in Canada alone.

The Canadian broadcasters are often complicit in the Americanization process. They know that an American appearance will not harm its attractiveness to Canadian audiences; all the most popular shows in English Canada are, in fact, American. Having the Americans involved also improves the budgets of the shows, enhancing their "production values" and making them more competitive.

Americanizing shows is very easy to do. The accents of Canadian actors are generally indistinguishable from American accents; the cities look much the same; and the narrative conventions of both countries are almost identical.

The problem is likely to become more severe as the Netflixes, Amazons, Hulus and Disneys come increasingly to dominate the Canadian broadcasting landscape. They may insist that the Canadian shows they buy from Canadian producers be acceptable to the US market. As of 2019 there was already anecdotal evidence that this was happening.

Creating Americanized shows is, of course, the absolute antithesis of the intended outcome. Government subsidies were not made available in order to produce ersatz Hollywood product. They were specifically intended to allow Canadians to make content that reflected Canada. When Canadian specificity is drained out, when American characters and cities are substituted, when stories are premised on American social and legal conventions, then the subsidy system becomes not just pointless, but downright destructive to Canada's own sense of itself.

The British, with a country almost twice as large as English Canada and a much longer cultural history, have taken a completely different approach to defining domestic content. The system, like Canada's, is based on points, but the points are awarded for different things. The system is culturally based. Of 35 points, the first 18 concern whether the characters are identifiably British, whether the program is clearly set in Britain, whether it is based on British subject matter and whether it is made in English. It then adds a further 4 points if the show is an interpretation of British culture, heritage or diversity. Only eight of the 35 points concern the creative team. The UK system pretty much guarantees that when a TV program or movie is made with British taxpayers' money, it looks, feels and smells like Britain.

The British rules apply not just to films and TV shows, but to videogames as well. The tax credit system does not distinguish between types of audio-visual content. It says simply that regardless of what is being produced, the products must be clearly and distinctly British if they are to be eligible for public funds.

While the adoption of the British system might cause some gnashing of teeth among the Canadian guilds and the producers, it would be a small price to pay to ensure that taxpayer money was spent to a real cultural end and not just to enrich producers or provide employment. The British rules do not seem to have disadvantaged British talent. The country's writers, directors and actors are more in demand than they have been in decades.

The upshot, then, is that if content is really to be king, the definition of Canadian content needs to change from an employment-based one to a culture-based one. The easiest way to proceed would be simply to adopt the UK rules. They are clear, proven and easy to administer.

After definition comes financing. If the purpose of a cultural policy is to finance Canadian content, then it seems odd to finance foreigners making foreign movies and TV shows in Canada. Yet the Production Services Tax Credit is precisely intended for that purpose. As of early 2019, it cost the Canadian government about $240 million per year — substantially more than the new tax credit the Liberal government has promised for news.[1]

Apart from the enormous amount of money involved, it seems slightly loony to subsidize our competitors. Now and in the future, Canadian shows and movies will be competing for international distribution, whether through conventional deals selling into foreign territories or to the new streaming services buying worldwide rights. If part of the government's policy is to encourage the export of Canadian culture (and it is), it hardly seems wise to finance the foreigners that are competing against us for international attention.

It is also not clear that the $240 million is necessary to attract foreign shoots to Canada. The real reason the Americans come here is because of the great crews and the value of the dollar. In fact, the difference on the exchange rate is worth much more than the subsidy. In 2016 and 2017, it was worth almost three times as much. They'll come as long as the dollar trades below 85 cents.

But even if they stopped coming, it would make little difference to the Canadian production services industry. As we shall see a little later, changes to the manner in which the foreign streaming services are regulated would inject an extra $1.4 billion into Canadian production.

The upshot, then, is that if Canadian content is king, we

need to stop subsidizing foreign content. Doing so will save considerable money that can be invested in Canadian shows and movies. That $240 million would go a long way to strengthening the production of Canadian content.

The second question to be asked is what Canadian content should be subsidized, who should help pay for it and who should be financed to make it?

A content-agnostic approach

Change is constant.

Changing technology makes new types of content possible. YouTube has created altogether new stars and transformed the reach of traditional ones. Lilly Singh's 15 million subscribers and Justin Bieber's billions of views would have been impossible without it.

A sensible cultural policy would be content-agnostic. It would be structured in such a way that the subsidy system evolves with the emergence of new forms that arise from changes in consumer taste, technological developments or shifts in market structure. It would not try to dictate what content is worthy and what is not.

The most glaring example of the inadequacies of the current system is the treatment of news. The government subsidizes much rubbish on TV. The morning shows are an endless blather of folksy chatter, sports scores, celebrity gossip and tips on what shoes to wear. Cooking and lifestyle shows receive funding. *Say Yes to the Dress* features women trying on wedding gowns; *Confucius was a Foodie* discusses Chinese food in North America. *Cabin Truckers*, in its fourth season in 2018, is a reality show that follows a family that puts cabins and other structures on trucks. These shows contribute nothing to our democracy or to the integrity of our governments.

The news, on the other hand, is what holds the responsible parties accountable when mayors feather their own nests, when city councillors employ their relatives, when powerful men harass vulnerable women, when financial advisors fleece their clients, when labs misdiagnose cancers, when big companies pollute rivers with mercury, when hospitals break down from overcrowding, when First Nations people live in unspeakable conditions. Without news, none of this would be revealed.

News is also the area that requires the most immediate attention because of the prevalence of its evil twin. As almost every commentator has noted, the best solution to false news is true news. The terrible irony is that the very platforms that are undermining true news are the very vehicles that allow the proliferation of hoaxes, trolling and falsehood.

In late 2016, Paul Godfrey called me and said that the study I had prepared for Rogers had been brought to his attention, and that he was very interested in its idea of tax credits for news. He asked if I would have dinner with his board and explain my proposal. A couple of weeks later, I did a briefing. It went well. The board members were enthusiastic — but then, Postmedia was getting desperate and was no doubt happy to hear any idea that might provide some relief.

After the dinner, Godfrey agreed to round up the other newspapers and see if they were prepared to finance a study on how tax credits might work for them. I asked John Cruickshank, the former publisher of the *Toronto Star*, and media economics expert Stephen Armstrong to join me in doing the work.

Over the next couple of weeks, almost all the newspapers agreed to join the group, as did the major magazine publishers. Torstar, *Le Devoir*, Transcontinental, Rogers Media,

St. Joseph's, the *Globe and Mail* and *La Presse* all met at Postmedia's boardroom to discuss how to work together. It was a strange gathering. Many of the publishers and CEOs actively disliked each other. They *all* disliked Paul Godfrey, who they blamed for giving them a bad reputation in Ottawa.

"Paul," one of them sniffed. "First he instructs his papers to support Stephen Harper and then every time he lays off some journalists, he gives himself a bonus. It makes us all look bad at the Prime Minister's Office."

Godfrey's explanation — that he had to accept a "stay" bonus as part of an agreement with his debt holders to take a haircut — evoked little sympathy from his colleagues.

Nevertheless, they were all in his boardroom, eyeing one another suspiciously. They listened to the explanation we gave about how the film and TV tax credits worked. We explained that if they were put in place for news, they would cover part of the labour costs involved in producing their newspapers and magazines. The salaries of the editors, journalists, graphic designers, photographers and layout artists — everyone involved in the production process, save management — would be eligible for the credits.

We explained, as well, that the tax-credit approach was best for news because it involved no judgements by politicians or bureaucrats. They were like any tax measure: If the costs qualified, the payment was automatic. This would safeguard the editorial independence of their papers and magazines.

The assembled press barons liked the approach and agreed to fund the research. They also agreed to open their books, so that we could understand their costs and estimate the size of the draw that a tax credit would make on the national treasury. We had to undertake, of course, that we would not share any of their cost information with their competitors around the table.

In January 2017, while the conversation on tax credits was going on, the Public Policy Forum released its report on the industry, *The Shattered Mirror*. It documented the perilous state of the newspapers' finances and proposed the creation of a Future of Democracy and Journalism Fund. Its role would be "to support digital news innovation — including technical strategies to make fake news less prominent — and civic function journalism, with a special emphasis on early stage local and indigenous news operations and research into issues relevant to the interaction of news and democracy."[2]

This somewhat amorphous proposal was hard to understand. It seemed to mix two quite different ideas: financing technical innovations of one variety or another, and subsidizing "civic function journalism," which the report defined as "the coverage of elected officials and public institutions, from legislatures, judicial or quasi-judicial bodies and city halls to school boards to supporting public services . . ."[3]

The newspapers did not much like the Public Policy Forum's recommendations. They had two fundamental objections.

First, they objected to the idea of a fund that they would have to apply to in order to receive financing. They were concerned that no matter how worthy the judicators of the fund, the approach could compromise their editorial independence. They feared that any process involving selective judgement could easily tip into favouring one point of view, one set of topics, one group of newspapers or one approach to making the digital transformation. For the publishers, it was essential that any support arrangements put in place had to be, and be seen to be, completely even-handed, without any possibility of political considerations entering the decision making.

Second, they found the concept of "civic journalism" too limiting. Their own papers and magazines covered a vast range of topics that went well beyond following elected officials and public institutions. They had whole sections of their publications that touched on everything from business and sports to culture and lifestyle. They offered book and movie reviews, financial advice, society gossip, profiles of famous personalities, obituaries, crossword puzzles, hockey scores, weather, horoscopes and on and on. The idea that they would be reduced to covering nothing but mayoralty races and library openings filled them with dread.

The author of the Pubic Policy Forum's report was Ed Greenspon. He had had a brilliant career in journalism. He had been the editor of the *Globe and Mail* and vice president of strategic investments for Star Media Group. He had tried to fashion his report in a way that he thought might be acceptable to the federal government. After it came out, he spent a considerable amount of time briefing the officials in Ottawa on its contents. He doubtless hoped, not surprisingly, that the report's recommendations would be implemented.

The problem that arose is that there were now two quite different proposals. There was the tax credit approach that the industry favoured and the fund/civic journalism idea that had the prestige of the Public Policy Forum behind it, as well as assurances from Greenspon that the mandarins in Ottawa did not like the idea of tax credits. The question then became how to square the circle.

This was becoming urgent since a meeting had been set up in early April 2017 for the industry to meet with the senior officials of the federal government to discuss how to move forward. The question was: Which approach? After much discussion, it was decided to brief the mandarins on both proposals, reviewing their pros and cons as we went. Although the magazines and newspapers preferred tax credits, they were happy to discuss the Public Policy Forum's ideas as well. If the mandarins really hated tax credits, then better the fund than nothing. As one of the publishers said to me, "At the end of the day, if the money has to be delivered in a brown paper bag late on Sunday nights in the alley, we'll take it." So the decision was taken to explain both approaches and let the officials decide. This would turn out to be a bad idea.

The meeting itself was extraordinary if for no other reason than it was the first time all the magazines and newspapers had been in the same room at the same time. They were accompanied by a senior official from Unifor, the labour union that represented most of their workers. The officials in attendance included many of the most senior people in the federal bureaucracy.

The reaction of the mandarinate reflected the cautious and slightly snooty quality of their somewhat insular culture. They are, by and large, extremely well-educated, holding advanced degrees from prestigious universities. They read books, go to the symphony, speak at least two languages, consume the *Economist* and the *New York Review of Books*, work very hard and have scant patience for people who like TV, rap music or any of the movies in the Marvel franchise.

From the outset of the conversation, it became clear that they would not be drawn into a debate on the merits of the two approaches, let alone endorse one. Rather, they spent their time exploring issues that seemed a little marginal.

"Okay," said a very senior mandarin. "But whatever form support might take, if any at all, it cannot be money for covering the Kardashians."

"No. No. Not the Kardashians," the others concurred.

It was a strange moment. They seemed not to know there was a vast sub-industry in Quebec concerned with nothing other than covering the French Canadian equivalent of the Kardashians. *Allô*, *Vedettes*, *7 Jours* and a raft of other magazines, websites and talk shows are devoted to Quebec's celebrity culture. It is, in fact, so vast and influential that it is the subject of regular, agonized hand-wringing on the part of the province's elites.

More importantly, the celebrity ecosystem in Quebec is fundamental to the extraordinary success enjoyed by French TV. The stars — the *vedettes* — appear in the *télé-romans* and talk shows, host the awards galas and are the backbone of *Tout le monde en parle*, where Mélanie Joly met her downfall. The celebrity culture in the province, like the vast celebrity universe in the United States, is key to the vibrancy of its popular culture. English Canada sadly lacks anything resembling such a star system.

After the tut-tutting about the Kardashians, there was some grousing about fake news and the usual genuflections to the importance of serious journalism. And then it was over. The publishers did not know quite what to make of the meeting. To the extent that conclusions could be drawn, it looked like a victory for civic journalism. They left baffled. Nothing specific was decided or resolved.

Days and weeks went by with no indication of next steps. Greenspon continued to take soundings in the higher echelons of the bureaucracy. He continued to report that there was no sympathy for tax credits. The boffins at finance hated the tax credits that already existed and wanted nothing to do with extending them to newspapers. Besides, the magazines were already at the trough; they had the Canada Periodical Fund.

The industry began to conclude that perhaps the credits would not fly and that it might be better to move over to the fund idea. Anything, after all, was better than nothing, even a paper bag full of money late on a Sunday evening.

In light of all the uncertainty, the newspapers' trade association, News Media Canada, made an attempt to break the logjam by proposing a compromise. They suggested that the Canada Periodical Fund be broadened to include a tax credit for newspapers. They suggested, as well, that the concept of "civic journalism" embrace any and all journalistic content.

Their ideas were not well-received by the magazine community, which saw the proposal to broaden the Periodical Fund as simply a raid on their limited money. They broke off their common front with the newspapers and decided to go their own way.

News Media Canada's ideas also failed to move the government. Mélanie Joly continued to talk about "failed business models" and nobody else seemed to care very much. This may have been because it was hard to make out exactly what the industry wanted. They said they wanted tax credits, but might settle for a fund; then again, maybe the fund should be the existing Periodical Fund. The newspapers were together with the magazines proposing a common approach; and then they were not.

This tangled process did have some virtues. It made clear, for one thing, that a couple of important principles need to be respected in thinking about support for the news business.

First and foremost, support must be at "arm's-length" from the government and automatic in its operation. The independence of the press requires that nobody except the editors decide what is or is not news. Creating funds that involve selective decision making is not compatible with this principle.

Second, the arrangements must be fair. The key question is how much money should be provided to the news business. The simplest answer is the same amount that is available to subsidize the costs of producing TV dramas, documentaries, movies and children's shows. The requirement to create a "content-agnostic" policy makes this essential. TV broadcasters should not be forced to choose drama over news because the subsidy for it is higher and their costs correspondingly lower.

As we noted earlier, the best way to accomplish all this is to provide labour tax credits for news in exactly the same way that is done for entertainment.

Chapter 1 related how, in Finance Minister Bill Morneau's 2018 fall economic update, the federal government announced a tax credit for the news industry. The decision got the principle of equal treatment right (up to a point). Where the update got it wrong is that the amount provided was too small. The sum of $45 million in 2019 would do almost nothing to assist the industry. The government also capped the amount of tax credits that could be drawn. This is not how it works for the entertainment credits; nor is it how it works for the credits that subsidize foreign shoots in Canada.

How much the TV and film tax credits cost the government varies from year to year depending on the volume of production. There are no arbitrary caps. If the amount goes up, it simply means — because they are labour-based — that more people are being hired. Increased demand and employment in the news business would be a welcome change from the last few years of endless layoffs.

To provide news with the same level of support as entertainment would cost the federal treasury about $430 million per year, $200 million for the papers, $30 million for magazines (over and above the existing Periodical Fund) and $200 million for TV news.[4] News subsidies paid in Europe put these figures in perspective. The French, for example, provide almost $1.5 billion a year to their newspaper industry in the forms of tax relief and cash. Adjusting for the fact that France has a population almost twice as large as Canada, an equivalent Canadian contribution would be about $780 million per year.

The good news is that tax credits are easy to administer. The machinery already exists at the Canadian Audio-Visual Certification Office, which has been administering the entertainment tax credits for years. There is no requirement to set up any new organization, pass new laws or create new funds.

The economic update failed, as well, to deal with the condition of the markets in which the news organizations operate. That Google and Facebook do not collect HST on their ad sales to Canadian companies gives them a significant competitive advantage over both the newspapers and the conventional TV networks. Nor do the foreign OTTs (Over The Tops) like Netflix charge HST. If the federal government were to require these foreign firms to charge HST, it would not only begin to level the playing field, it would also yield at least $100 million to the treasury.[5]

Beyond the HST issue, both Google and Facebook enjoy

the benefits of Bill C-58, despite the fact that they are not Canadian-owned and -controlled. This is the result of a technical loophole. The effect of it, however, is to let Canadian companies deduct their advertising expenses with Google and Facebook as legitimate business expenses for tax purposes. The loophole, thus, subverts the entire purpose of C-58, which was to ensure that Canadian advertising revenues remained in Canada and stayed with Canadian media companies.

Eliminating this loophole, so that Canadian companies could not deduct their advertising costs with foreign digital ad sellers as a legitimate business expense, could yield considerable benefits. If the same level of revenues were repatriated that flowed back to Canadian companies from the border broadcasters and *Time* in the 1970s, as much as $1.3 billion would be returned to the TV and newspaper companies.[6]

On those revenues that were not repatriated, the treasury would enjoy a windfall gain, since the advertising expenses remaining with Google and Facebook would no longer be tax exempt. This would yield an additional $590 million in corporate taxes paid to the federal government. If no money was repatriated, because Canadian advertisers wanted to stay with Google and Facebook and were prepared to forego the tax advantages, the treasury would enjoy a windfall of almost $800 million.

Bringing the FAANGs within the existing tax rules, making them collect HST and be subject to C-58, would go some distance to restoring the perimeter of the garden. Along with the elimination of the production services tax credit, it would also provide the federal government with about $1 billion in uncommitted tax revenues, more than twice as much as it would need to provide the same level of support to Canadian news that it now provides to Canadian entertainment.

Providing news production of whatever variety, TV, papers or magazines, with the same support as drama, documentaries and kids' shows — the roughly $430 million per year described earlier — would provide not only significantly more room to make the digital transition that they are already working on, it might also create opportunities to bring back papers and shows that had been cancelled in the last many years of aggressive cost cutting.

A platform-agnostic approach

The *Broadcasting Act* provides that all broadcasters in Canada, whether they be conventional over-the-air broadcasters, specialty channels, video-on-demand services, or cable or satellite TV companies, must be Canadian-owned and -controlled. Netflix, Amazon, CBS All Access are clearly broadcasters. They do exactly what CTV and Global do: They buy and commission TV shows. When Disney, Time Warner and the rest begin offering streaming services in Canada, they, too, will be broadcasters under the *Act*.

The only reason that they are allowed to operate in Canada is because of the Digital Media Exemption Order — the hole in the garden wall that the CRTC put in place in 1999 and reconfirmed as recently as 2015. To rebuild the garden for TV requires having the foreign broadcasters behave as proper corporate citizens like any other foreign-owned company operating in Canada. What form should this take?

The CRTC's report to Mélanie Joly on the subject, *Harnessing Change: The Future of Programming Distribution in Canada*, discussed the issue at length.

It started off sensibly, by saying that for the FAANGs, "there are social and cultural responsibilities with operating in Canada and [we need] to ensure that all players benefiting from Canada and Canadians participate in appropriate and equitable . . . ways to benefit Canadians and Canada."[7] Nobody could quibble with that.

Unfortunately, it then wandered into strange territory. It took the view that the new foreign streaming services were so different from traditional broadcasting that "Applying regulatory approaches developed for traditional TV and radio to these online players is unlikely to maximise benefits for Canadians."

Why this was the case the commission did not really say. It noted, for example, that when Amazon offers TV programs, it does so as part of a speedy delivery service that people pay for on a monthly basis. This, the CRTC claimed, made Amazon's television service radically different from traditional broadcasters. It was a strange argument, since Amazon does what all broadcasters do: It commissions shows and makes them available to the public.

In much of its reasoning, the CRTC seemed to want to avoid the duck test. Despite Netflix and the others quacking loudly, laying eggs and paddling around in the great pond of Canada, the commissioners did not want to call them ducks. This was particularly surprising, since the CRTC had found consistently over the last twenty years that the new digital platforms and what they did was, in fact, broadcasting and they were, in fact, ducks. That is why it had to update its digital media exemption every five years or so.

The CRTC's failure to see that it was dealing with ducks led it into many odd places. It concluded, as a result, that the current licensing system is neither nimble nor flexible enough to deal with these exotic and previously unknown creatures. It believed that a new approach was required, in which regulations of general application would be replaced with "comprehensive and binding service agreements." Each company's agreement would be based on incentives and be tailored to suit its specific and unique characteristics. Netflix might have one kind of agreement, Amazon another, Facebook a third and Disney/Fox something different again. The danger in all this is that it begins to resemble the Baie-Comeau policy for publishing, where everyone ended up with a different deal. Inevitably this led to charges — correctly — that the policy was arbitrary.

It is also not clear why Netflix or Disney would agree to enter into these "comprehensive and binding service agreements." What does the commission do if they simply say "no thank you"? What then? Unless it is prepared to impose some sanctions, it's hard to see why anyone would bother to negotiate, let alone agree.

There is a much simpler way through the problem. Netflix and the others should be subject to the same rules as CTV and Global. They should have to spend 30 per cent of their previous year Canadian gross revenues on Canadian TV shows and movies. Requiring them do so would have them spend $438 million in 2020.[8]

In fairness to the foreign streaming services, requiring them to spend 30 per cent of their gross revenues on Canadian content should also entitle their productions access to the TV tax credits and the Canada Media Fund/Telefilm. If they did, they would draw about $150 million in credits and the same amount again from the Canada Media Fund/Telefilm, requiring a total of $300 million be made available. Altogether, this would trigger about $1.4 billion in new Canadian production.[9]

The new $300 million that is required should not be hard to finance. Even after providing funding for the news tax credit ($430 million), there will still be about $600 million in new uncommitted tax revenues left from the $1 billion raised by applying the HST rules and Section 19.1 of the *Income Tax Act* to foreign digital media.

Having Netflix and the other foreigners invest in Canadian shows will make it all the more important to convert the Canadian content rules to the UK system. This will ensure that the shows they commission are genuinely Canadian, that they look, feel, taste and smell like Canada. If this does not happen, the danger, as noted earlier, is that the foreign companies will commission American shows made with Canadian talent.

Netflix may object that it should not have to spend 30 per cent of its Canadian gross revenues, since they already made a deal with Mélanie Joly to spend $100 million each year over five years. It is hard to know what to say about this argument. Joly claimed herself, after she got walloped, that the $100 million was "transitional." Perhaps that is so, but it is impossible to say, since the deal between the government and Netflix has never been made public.

More broadly, a 30 per cent rule is consistent with what the Europeans have required of any and all platforms that provide audio-visual content. They must have 30 per cent European content and they must "ensure prominence of those works." The 30 per cent rule has a nice symmetry. It puts Netflix on the same footing as its Canadian competitors and makes Canada's rules congruent with those of the European Union.

There is, however, one area where a major concession can and should be made to Netflix and the others. They can be exempted from the ownership requirements of the *Broadcasting Act*. They need not be forced to divest their businesses in Canada to Canadians as Paramount and Famous Players had to do in 1969. This would be a very significant concession.

If these arrangements were put in place, the Americans would have no grounds on which to complain. Netflix and the rest would have to play by the same rules as their Canadian counterparts, have access to the same subsidies, but not have to change their ownership structure. This is better than the "national treatment" test in the North American Free Trade Agreement, which requires that US companies operating in Canada be treated as well as their Canadian counterparts. The national treatment test will presumably also be required by the new United States-Canada-Mexico Agreement.

Like the tax credits, this policy is easy to put in place. It does not require new legislation, new funds, or new anything else. The government can implement it simply by giving a directive to the CRTC under its powers in the existing *Act*.

A producer-agnostic approach

Only "independent" producers qualify for tax credits and the Canada Media Fund. Independent producers are defined as production houses that are not owned and controlled by broadcasters or film distributors. They are the only ones who qualify to make movies or shows in the most popular genres. Producers "affiliated" with a broadcaster cannot access these funds, except in an extremely limited way.

This makes the Canadian production infrastructure for TV and films very strange. As we saw in Chapter 3, the independent producers are by and large quite small, undercapitalized companies. They are mostly too little to take significant risks or manage large projects.

Canada's biggest competitors do not structure themselves this way. In both the US and the UK, the major networks all have affiliated production companies. BBC has BBC studios; ABC has Disney; NBC has NBCUniversal. This allows those who have the greatest financial interest in the success of a show to be able to make sure they succeed with audiences and foreign sales.

It also ensures that there are companies big enough to handle the complex risks involved in program production and export. In the US, for every five scripts that are purchased, only one will be made into a pilot; and for every twenty pilots made, only six will go on-air; and of those, only two will last more than a single season. The economics of the business require, therefore, that companies have a large portfolio of projects. They must be big enough to fail frequently, so that they can ultimately succeed.[10]

The inability of Canadian broadcasters to work like their British and American counterparts puts them at a significant disadvantage. When their advertising revenues are eroding and their cable fees are shrinking, the most obvious place for them to look for new revenues is in program production. But because of the rules governing the subsidy system, they cannot go there.

The situation of Corus illustrates the problem. Its focus is on programming for women and children. In 2000, it bought Nelvana, one of Canada's most important producers of kids' shows. The plan was to have Corus's children's TV networks — Treehouse, Teletoon, YTV and Nickelodeon Canada — commission shows from Nelvana. This would have allowed Nelvana to work closely with the broadcasters who understood the market best and, at the same time, it would have provided the channels with programs from their own production house. This would have been good for both Corus's TV networks and Nelvana.

More broadly, this would have given Corus an opportunity to diversify its revenue streams as the advertising revenues and cable fees that it relies on decline. It would, as well, have given the company the critical mass that it would need to be globally competitive in producing TV shows. Unfortunately, the plan could never be fully realized because Nelvana is an affiliated production company and the rules favouring independent producers have never been changed.

For its part, Bell Media would also like to be able to move more heavily into production. It has been buying studios and has started investing in musicals, but it faces the same limitations as Corus: It cannot use its TV networks to commission from an affiliated producer. Bell, too, will be thwarted in its ambitions unless the rule is changed.

In a world where production of movies and TV shows is increasingly dominated by some of the biggest companies in the world — by Amazon, Apple, Disney/Fox, Comcast/ NBCUniversal and AT&T/Time-Warner — it seems unwise to insist that our production houses remain small and undercapitalized. The better course is to let the (relatively) big media groups in Canada lever all of their resources to see whether it is possible to build internationally competitive companies.

The change in the rule would not apply to the operations of the foreign streaming services in Canada. They would be exempt from the requirement to be Canadian-owned and -controlled, but they would have to commission their Canadian shows from Canadian-owned and -controlled producers. Their 30 per cent of gross revenues would have to be spent on Canadian shows made by Canadian companies.

There is no reason why they should object to this. The Canadian production infrastructure is one of the best in the world. Moreover, if the broadcasters' affiliated production companies are allowed access to the full array of support measures, they will have a greater number of production companies to choose from.

Providing the broadcasters with an opportunity to diversify into production is no guarantee that they will survive. They are in a perilous state. They may still die. The change will, however, make it more likely that a viable, globally competitive Canadian production industry will survive.

The injection of significant new money — the $1.4 billion from the FAANGs — will give Canadian producers, both affiliated and unaffiliated, a significant shot in the arm. Having the foreign broadcasters commission Canadian shows will give those shows access to the largest distribution networks in the world. When Netflix and Disney buy programs here, they will also make them available throughout the rest of their empires. Our Canadian shows will be seen in Europe and South America, in Asia and Africa. That alone will be a good thing.

Finally, beyond making a new cultural policy agnostic with respect to content, platforms and producers, it needs to ensure that the new digital platforms contribute to the strengthening of Canadian democracy and civil discourse. This will require that rules be put to make the FAANGs responsible for the content they carry.

Here the Europeans have led the way. Their reasoning is straightforward: The FAANGs are media companies and need to be treated like media companies. The recent changes to European law will require the Facebooks and YouTubes to take measures against content "inciting violence, hatred and terrorism." They will be bound by the traditional standards that apply to broadcasters and journalists.

The new rules of the European Union are laid out in detail in its Code of Practice on Disinformation that came into force in the fall of 2018. Both Google and Facebook have signed on to them. Fortunately for Canada, the Europeans have done a great deal of heavy lifting on how to approach these problems. Like the UK point system, the Code on Disinformation provides the federal government with a model that has already been worked out in detail and accepted by the FAANGs.

In Canada, similar standards have been in place for a long time. The Canadian Association of Broadcasters' Code of Ethics has been in place for years and everyone in the industry accepts it. The key provision is that "broadcasters shall ensure that their programming contains no abusive or unduly discriminatory material or comment which is based on matters of race, national or ethnic origin, colour, age, sexual orientation, marital status or physical or mental disability." This pretty much covers hate speech, ethnic slurs and race-baiting.[11]

The code also deals with fake news. It says that "it shall be the responsibility of the broadcasters to ensure that news shall be represented with accuracy and without bias." The code incorporates the Radio, Television, Digital News Association's Code of Journalistic Ethics, which states that broadcasters are committed to news that is "accurate and reliable . . . and . . . will strive to verify facts . . ." The same duties attach to newspapers.

The FAANGs will not have a choice about whether or not to accept these codes. Once the Digital Media Exemption Order is removed by the CRTC and they are treated as broadcasters, they will, like all broadcasters, have to abide by the codes.

Some commentators have objected that insisting on these codes will put Facebook in the position of having to make decisions about what kind of speech is allowed and what is not. They say that should be a matter for the courts, not for the Silicon Valley behemoths. Putting them in that position could restrict freedom of expression.

This is a curious objection. The code seems to have worked well for TV and radio. Canada does not seem to be particularly restrictive with respect to freedom of expression. Reporters Without Borders perennially ranks Canada in the top twenty countries for freedom of expression, significantly ahead of the United States, France and the UK. We are also, unlike the US, not awash in race-baiting and fake news.

Others have pointed out that Facebook alone has more than 2 billion users, all merrily posting away. Purely as a practical matter, it will be very difficult, if not impossible, for Facebook to monitor everything that goes on the platform.

Again, this seems a strange concern. Facebook already does it for child pornography and terrorist videos. It just needs to extend its efforts. It will have to do so in any event, since this is precisely the approach that the Europeans have taken. They have simply said that they are broadcasters and must abide by their broadcast codes. Facebook can hardly object if we do the same.

Besides, the fact that it is a problem and an expense for Facebook is surely not the Government of Canada's problem. If it costs Facebook a lot of money, if it impairs its share price, if it even drives it into bankruptcy, it is not the Government of Canada's problem. The government's duty is to maintain the integrity of our democracy, not to worry about Facebook's financial performance. Besides, it seems clear that Facebook has the resources to do this job; it is, after all, one of the largest and wealthiest companies in the world.

CONCLUSION

Much is at stake. The common threads that bind us together are fraying. When the media fail, we lose the major vehicle that allows us to converse among ourselves; we lose, in effect, the ongoing national discussion that makes sense of our lives as citizens and Canadians.

The erosion of the financial underpinnings of the newspaper and television businesses is far advanced. If they collapse, we are in danger of being left only with the vast digital platforms of Facebook, Netflix and Google. We will fall not into a richer, bigger, more international conversation; rather we will fall out of our own media ecosystem into one that is increasingly dominated by trolls and hoaxes, filter bubbles and fake news. We will fall into a smaller, meaner world.

None of this is inevitable. If the measures described in Chapter 7 are put in place, we should be able to ensure the future integrity of Canadian culture. They are measures designed not to exclude the FAANGs, but to ensure that they contribute fairly to the support of the national conversation, as the traditional media have done for more than a hundred years.

The measures are neither novel nor strange. They are, in fact, simply extensions of the rules that have historically governed the broadcasting and newspaper businesses. They require that the FAANGs be subject to the same tax regimes as the traditional media, that they make the same contributions to the production of Canadian content and respect the same standards of civility and truthfulness that bind the newspapers and broadcasters. In return, they should be allowed to access the same support measures as their Canadian counterparts.

Most of these measures are already in place in Europe and many other countries. They are not punitive, discriminatory or unfair. They are, in fact, completely consistent with the principle of national treatment. The FAANGs in Europe are subject to the same rules as their European counterparts and enjoy the same protections.

Requiring Netflix and Amazon to contribute to the creation of Canadian content, and to feature it in their recommendation engines, may also establish useful precedents for the book and music industries. Spotify and Apple Music are streaming services like Netflix and Amazon. While they do not commission or produce music themselves, it would not be unreasonable to require them to provide Canadian options to Canadians when they make recommendations. For every ten songs, albums or artists they recommend, three might be Canadian.

In books, Audible has already agreed to this principle. When Canadians go to select an audiobook, Audible will recommend Canadian ones, as well as others from around the world. Requiring Amazon to do the same thing for printed books and e-books would be a good idea, particularly since Amazon owns Audible.

There are no guarantees that the measures outlined above will save the newspapers or the broadcasters. Tax credits for news will help the companies make the digital transition; they will buy some time and breathing space. Ultimately, however, it will be up to the companies themselves to reinvent the news in a way that makes it relevant, compelling and accessible to a new generation of Canadians.

Allowing the broadcasters to produce movies and TV shows with full access to the tax credits, the Canada Media Fund and Telefilm will allow them to create a new revenue stream to mitigate what they are losing in advertising revenues. It will also put them on the same footing as their American and British competitors.

Requiring Netflix, Amazon and the rest to spend 30 per cent of their gross revenues on Canadian content will not guarantee the future of the broadcasting system. It will, however, level the playing field, so that Canadian companies are not operating at a disadvantage in their home market. Ensuring equality of treatment seems the very least that should be done.

At the same time, having Netflix and the others make that outlay will inject significant new funds into the film and TV production industries, with the result that many more Canadian films and television shows will be produced. If they are made using a UK-type points system, they will, as well, be distinctly Canadian. They will be Canadian content that is clearly about Canada and features Canadian locations, stories, characters and settings.

Finally, requiring Google and Netflix to monitor the content on their platforms following the same standards as Canadian broadcasters and newspapers is neither discriminatory nor an abrogation of freedom of expression. It should significantly reduce the level of fake news, trolling and hate speech that pollutes them now. The Europeans have already insisted on this measure. There is no reason why Canada cannot do so as well.

The financial resources required to give effect to these new measures can be found without increasing the draw on the treasury. Simply extending the sales tax, abolishing the tax credits for foreign shoots and eliminating the loophole on the application of C-58 will generate sufficient funds. Doing so will not only generate the necessary money, it will also level the playing field for Canadian media and obviate the need to raise new taxes on, as has been suggested in many quarters, internet service providers.

If these changes in policy are to be made, however, they must be made now. The financial situation of the traditional media is so fragile that they cannot wait much longer.

Unfortunately, the government has attempted to tie its own hands well into the future. It seems to believe that it cannot act unless it rewrites the *various* acts that underpin the regulation of these industries. To figure out how to do this, it has established a Broadcasting and Telecommunications Legislation Review Panel to tell it how to do so. The panel will not report until 2020.

Once it has reported, the government will have to consider its recommendations, discuss them at cabinet, draft new legislation, take it through the three readings in the House and Senate and then get royal assent. The most optimistic observers do not believe that this can be done in less than three years. A very distinguished communications lawyer believes that it could take as long as seven years. By then, there is likely to be no Canadian industry left to save.

Happily, it is not necessary to await the passage of new

legislation before acting. All the measures proposed in this book can be put in place using the legislative powers the government already has.

There is no reason why Canadian culture cannot flourish in the digital age. It simply requires that the government adapt the historic garden policies and draw the FAANGs into the existing network of taxes, regulations and standards. If it does so, there is every reason to be hopeful about the future.

Every generation of Canadians has had to struggle to avoid being culturally assimilated into the mighty power to the south. The governments of Robert Borden, William Lyon Mackenzie King, John Diefenbaker, Lester Pearson, Brian Mulroney and Jean Chrétien all had to address the issue. The technologies and problems were different from one to another, but the will was always the same. Despite frequent threats and pushback from the Americans, they moved continuously forward, striving always to ensure that Canada remained Canadian. This generation can surely do no less.

ACKNOWLEDGEMENTS

Thank you to many friends and colleagues who provided comments and suggestions on various drafts of the book. In particular, I would like to thank Claude Galipeau, David Watt, Jeremy Kinsman, Catherine Tait, Daniel Weinzweig, Jim Mitchell and Heaton Dyer. Special thanks goes to Alex Piitz our wonderful and conscientious research assistant. Needless to say, the views expressed in the book do not necessarily reflect their views and all errors are those of the authors.

ENDNOTES

Introduction

1. George Grant, *Lament for a Nation* (Toronto: McClelland and Stewart, 1965), 4.

Chapter 1

1. ThinkTV, "Reach & Time Spent: Major Media Comparison Canada 2015–2016 Broadcast Year," 2015. (See Table 1.)

Table 1: Weekly Per Capita Hours, TV and Internet, by Age Group, Canada, 2015/16					
	18–24	18–34	18–49	25–54	55+
TV	16.7	17.7	19.5	21.8	38.7
Internet	25.3	24.8	24.7	25.4	11.70

2. "And the World's Most Popular Websites Are . . ." *CBC*, October 3, 2013, www.cbc.ca/strombo/news/the-most-visited-websites-by-country; "Top Sites in Canada," Alexa, 1 Month Rank, December 2018. In October 2013, the CBC reported that of the top 25 websites in Canada, only two were Canadian: the Government of Canada website and TD Canada Trust. As of December 2018, only three Canadian websites had made it into the top 25 — two Canadian banks (TD and RBC) and Pornhub, an aggregator of online pornography. (The one month rank is calculated using a combination of average daily website visitors and pageviews over the past month. The site with the highest combination of visitors and pageviews is ranked #1.)

3. ThinkTV, "Net Advertising Volume." December 11, 2018, thinktv.ca/research/advertising-revenue-by-media/. (See Table 2.)

Table 2: Reported Media Net Advertising Revenues, Canada, 2007 to 2017, $M											
	2007	2008	2009	2010	2011	2012	2013	2014	2015	2016	2017
TV	3,299	3,393	3,104	3,391	3,682	3,614	3,537	3,511	3,345	3,327	3,195
	30.8%	29.9%	29.3%	29.7%	30.8%	29.1%	29.2%	29.1%	27.0%	25.8%	23.5%
Newspaper	3,875	3,880	3,429	3,491	3,427	3,550	2,936	2,590	2,305	2,133	1,777
	36.2%	34.2%	32.4%	30.5%	28.7%	28.6%	24.3%	21.4%	18.6%	16.6%	13.1%
Internet	1,243	1,609	1,845	2,279	2,674	3,085	3,418	3,793	4,604	5,485	6,771
	11.6%	14.2%	17.4%	19.9%	22.4%	24.8%	28.2%	31.4%	37.1%	42.6%	49.8%
Total	10,705	11,348	10,584	11,433	11,944	12,418	12,106	12,077	12,399	12,871	13,584

Nordicity, "The Digital Media Universe in Canada: Measuring the Revenues, the Audiences, and the Future Prospects," Toronto: Faculty of Music, University of Toronto, 2018. (See Table 3.)

Table 3: Share of Internet Ad Revenues, Canada, 2016

Google	48.0%
Facebook	23.9%
Google + Facebook	71.9%
Yellow Pages	2.5%
Torstar	2.4%
Postmedia	2.0%
Quebecor	0.4%
Globe & Mail	0.4%
Other	20.7%

4. CRTC, *Communications Monitoring Report 2017* (Ottawa: Canadian Radio-television and Telecommunications Commission, 2017), https://crtc.gc.ca/eng/publications/reports/PolicyMonitoring/2017/cmr2017.pdf; Media Technology Monitor (MTM), cited in "Market Insights: Audience Trends, Part 1, Figure 1" in *Harnessing Change: The Future of Programming Distribution in Canada* (Ottawa: Canadian Radio-television and Telecommunications Commission, 2018), https://crtc.gc.ca/eng/publications/s15/mar1.htm; Statistics Canada, "Dwelling Counts, for Canada, Provinces and Territories, 2016 and 2011 Censuses — 100% Data" last modified February 8, 2018, https://www12.statcan.gc.ca/census-recensement/2016/dp-pd/hlt-fst/pd-pl/Table.cfm?Lang=Eng&T=108&S=50&O=A. Calculations provided by Armstrong Consulting. (See Table 4.)

Table 4: Estimated Netflix Subscribers, Revenues and Penetration, Canada, 2012 to 2016

	2012	2013	2014	2015	2016
Revenues ($M)	162	258	454	638	766
Subscribers (M)	1.4	2.1	3.8	5.3	6.4
Total HH (M)	13.5	13.6	13.8	13.9	14.1
Penetration	10.0%	15.8%	27.5%	30.0%	45.4%

Notes:

- Netflix revenues are assumed to equal 70 per cent of total subscription video on-demand (SVOD) revenues in Canada, as was the case in 2016 as per CRTC estimates. Subscriber estimates assume an average monthly rate of $10.

5. Statistics Canada, "Dwelling Counts, for Canada, Provinces and Territories, 2016 and 2011 Censuses – 100% Data"; CRTC, *Broadcasting Procedural Letter Addressed to Various Parties*, Ottawa, May 11, 2018. CRTC, *Broadcasting Distribution, Statistical and Financial Summaries, 2013 to 2017*. CRTC reports are available online: *open.canada.ca/data/en/dataset/5032ef1f-bc28-4e8d-8a96-9eed77f29d99*. Calculations provided by Armstrong Consulting. (See Table 5.)

Table 5: Total Households, BDU Subscribers and Non-BDU Households, Canada, 2012 to 2017, 000s

	2012	2013	2014	2015	2016	2017
Total HH Canada	13,467	13,615	13,765	13,916	14,072	14,227
Total BDU Subscribers	11,461	11,440	11,296	11,147	10,907	10,703
% of Total HH	85.1%	84.0%	82.1%	80.1%	77.5%	75.2%
Change +/-	64	-21	-144	-149	-239	-205
Non BDU HH	2,006	2,175	2,469	2,770	3,165	3,524
% of Total HH	14.9%	16.0%	17.9%	19.9%	22.5%	24.8%

MTM, cited in "Market Insights" in *Harnessing Change*, CRTC, rs 2018. (See Table 6.)

Table 6: BDU Penetration by English and French-Language Markets

	2010	2011	2012	2013	2014	2015	2016	2017
English Language Markets	86%	87%	85%	84%	82%	77%	75%	73%
French Language Markets	90%	89%	89%	90%	90%	89%	87%	83%

6. Statistics Canada, "Newspaper Publishers, Summary Statistics: Table 21-10-0191-01" last modified January 10, 2019, www150.statcan.gc.ca/t1/tbl1/en/tv.action?pid=2110019101; Statistics Canada, "Periodical Publishers, Summary Statistics: Table 21-10-0053-01" last modified January 10, 2019, www150.statcan.gc.ca/t1/tbl1/en/tv.action?pid=2110005301. (See Table 7.)

Table 7: Newspaper and Periodical Operating Revenues, 2014 and 2016, Canada, $B

			Per cent
	2014	2016	Change
Newspaper	4.0	3.2	-20%
			Per cent
	2013	2015	Change
Periodicals	2.0	1.6	-18%

7. CRTC, "Aggregate Annual Returns for Large Broadcasters pursuant to Broadcasting Regulatory Policy CRTC 2009-560," 2011–2017,crtc.gc.ca/eng/industr/ann.htm (See Table 8)

Table 8: Private Conventional Television Groups, Revenues and Profits/Losses, 2011–2017, $M								
		2011	2012	2013	2014	2015	2016	2017
Bell Media	Revenues	$837	$811	$776	$736	$724	$717	$675
	PBIT	$58	$(15)	$3	$(39)	$(24)	$(33)	$(33)
Corus	Revenues	$522	$447	$417	$404	$405	$371	$346
	PBIT	$35	$23	$(6)	$(25)	$(29)	$(43)	$(56)
Rogers	Revenues	$298	$291	$273	$228	$222	$198	$206
	PBIT	$(0)	$(41)	$(49)	$(85)	$(83)	$(35)	$(16)
Quebecor	Revenues	$260	$257	$249	$229	$214	$209	$219
	PBIT	$36	$25	$25	$0	$(3)	$1	$6
Remstar	Revenues	$66	$73	$77	$67	$67	$61	$47
	PBIT	$3	$0	$1	$(3)	$4	$2	$(4)
Total Group	Revenues	$1,984	$1,878	$1,792	$1,665	$1,632	$1,556	$1,493
	PBIT	$132	$(7)	$(26)	$(151)	$(135)	$(108)	$(104)

8. Daniel Leblanc, "Everything's on the Table," *Globe and Mail*, April 23, 2016, www.theglobeandmail.com/news/national/exclusive-canadian-heritage-announces-sweeping-canconreview/article29722581/.

9. Statistics Canada, "Provincial and Territorial Culture Indicators 2016: Economic Importance of Culture and Sport in Canada," *Daily*, February 27 2018, www150.statcan.gc.ca/n1/daily-quotidien/180227/dq180227a-eng.htm.

10. Statistics Canada, "Labour Force Characteristics by Industry, Annual (x 1,000): Table 14-0023-01" last modified January 10, 2019, www150.statcan.gc.ca/t1/tbl1/en/tv.action?pid=1410002301. (See Table 9.)

Table 9: Employment by Sector, Canada, 2016, 000s/%		
	#	%
Culture	652	3.5%
Agriculture	280	1.5%
Forestry, logging and support activites for forestry	48	0.3%
Fishing, hunting and trapping	17	0.1%
Total	345	1.9%
Mining, quarrying, oil and gass extraction	264	1.4%
Total Employment	18,416	100%

11. Richard Stursberg, *Cultural Policy for the Digital Age*, 2016, https://techlaw. uottawa.ca/sites/techlaw.uottawa.ca/files/culturalpolicyforthedigitalage.pdf.

12. Public Policy Forum, *The Shattered Mirror: News, Democracy And Trust in the Digital Age* (Ottawa: Public Policy Forum, January 2017), https:// shatteredmirror.ca.

13. *Shattered Mirror*, 4.

14. *Shattered Mirror*, 38.

15. *Shattered Mirror*, 88.

16. United Kingdom House of Commons Culture, Media and Sport Committee, *Future for Local and Regional Media*, Fourth Report of Session 2009–2010, vol. 1, April 6, 2010, 9, as cited in Standing Committee on Canadian Heritage, *Disruption: Change and Churning in Canada's Media Landscape*, 42nd Parliament, First Session, June 2017, p.6, www.ourcommons.ca/Content/Committee/421/CHPC/Reports/RP9045583/chpcrp06/chpcrp06-e.pdf.

17. www.canada.ca/en/canadian-heritage/campaigns/creative-canada/framework.html.

18. CRTC, *Communications Monitoring Report 2017*; MTM, cited in "Market Insights" in *Harnessing Change*, CRTC, 2018. Estimates based on publicly available data generally confirm the initial analyses of the Netflix deal. Calculations provided by Armstrong Consulting. (See Table 10)

Table 10: Estimated Netflix Revenues in Canada, Canadian Program Expenditure as Agreed and at 30% of Revenues, $M

	2016	2017	2018	2019	2020	2021	
Estimated Revenues	766	895	965	1,015	1,067	1,120	
Agreed Expenditure		100	100	100	100	100	
Expenditure at 30%		230	269	289	305	320	Total
Difference		-130	-169	-189	-205	-220	-913

Notes:

• Revenue projections assume that the annual rate of growth decreases significantly over the projection period as the penetration of the Netflix service in Canada matures.

• The 30% expenditure requirement is calculated based on previous year revenues.

19. Mélanie Joly, interview, *Tout le monde en parle*, October 1, 2017.

20. Robert Everett-Green, "A Stunning Fall from Grace for Mélanie Joly," *Globe and Mail*, October 4, 2017, www.theglobeandmail.com/opinion/a-stunning-fall-from-grace-for-melanie-joly/article36497712/. 21. Canadian Heritage,

Creative Canada Policy Framework (Gatineau, Que.: Canadian Heritage, 2017), 26, www.canada.ca/en/canadian-heritage/campaigns/creative-canada/framework.html.

22. *Shattered Mirror*, 44.

23. *Shattered Mirror*, 15.

24. Susan Krashinsky Robertson and Daniel Leblanc, "Ottawa Not to Blame for Newspaper Closings: Joly," *Globe and Mail*, November 28, 2017, www.theglobeandmail.com/report-on-business/ottawa-not-to-blame-for-newspaper-closings-joly/article37121785/.

25. Mylene Crete, and Jordan Press, "Ottawa Poised to Help Newspapers in Coming Federal Budget," *National Post*, January 26, 2018, https://nationalpost.com/pmn/news-pmn/canada-news-pmn/ottawa-poised-to-help-newspapers-in-upcoming-budget.

26. "Ottawa Poised to Help Newspapers in Coming Federal Budget."

27. Canadian Press. "Mélanie Joly Says a Potential Netflix Tax Is Not Her Department," *Montreal Gazette*, December 8, 2017, https://montrealgazette.com/business/melanie-joly-says-shes-listening-to-quebecers-on-netflix-tax.

28. Canadian Press, "Bill Morneau Says Ottawa Has No Plans for a Netflix Tax," *Globe and Mail*, December 10, 2017, www.theglobeandmail.com/news/politics/bill-morneau-insists-trudeau-government-has-no-plans-for-a-netflix-tax/article37286169/.

29. John Honderich, "John Honderich: We Should All Be Very Concerned by the Crisis Facing Quality Journalism," *Toronto Star*, January 26, 2018, www.thestar.com/opinion/2018/01/26/john-honderich-we-should-all-be-very-concerned-by-the-crisis-facing-quality-journalism.html.

30. Justin Trudeau, 42nd Parliament, 1st Session. February 5, 2018.

31. CRTC, Harnessing Change: The Future of Programming Distribution in Canada. CRTC, 2018 (crtc.gc.ca/eng/publications/s15/).

32. Postmedia and Torstar, *Annual and Quarterly Reports, 2014 to 2018*, Quarterly reports are available on the Postmedia and Torstar websites, calculations provided by Armstrong Consulting. (See Table 11.)

Table 11: Postmedia and Torstar, Revenues and Operating Income, Actual and Projected, 2014 to 2020, $M

		2014A	2015A	2016A	2017A	2018A/P	2019P	2020P
Postmedia	Revenues	674	750	860	754	676	606	544
	Op. Inc	-36	-148	-280	-47	-9	-69	-132
Torstar	Revenues	858	787	685	616	531	459	396
	Op. Inc	-44	-354	-61	-18	-26	-99	-162
Post + Tor	Revenues	1,532	1,537	1,545	1,370	1,208	1,065	940
	Op. Inc	-80	-502	-341	-65	-35	-168	-294

Notes:

- Revenues and operating income for Postmedia 2014 to 2018 are actuals. Revenues and operating income for Torstar 2014 to 2017 are actuals and in 2018 are a projection based on data for the first three quarters of that year.

- Projections for Postmedia and Torstar for 2019 and 2020 assume that revenues for the two companies decrease in 2019 and 2020 at the same rate as the decrease from 2017 to 2018 (-10.3 per cent and -13.7 per cent respectively) and that costs remain constant.

33. CRTC, *Conventional Television, Statistical and Financial Summaries, 2013 to 2017* (open.canada.ca/data/en/dataset/5032ef1f-bc28-4e8d-8a96-9eed77f29d99); CRTC, Broadcasting Notice of Consultation CRTC 2017-428, December 5 2017 (https://crtc.gc.ca/eng/archive/2017/2017-428.htm) *Conventional TV Groups, Financial Projections, Group TV Licence Renewal Applications, Reconsideration*, calculations provided by Armstrong Consulting. (See Table 12.)

Table 12: Private Conventional Television, Revenues and Profit, 2013 to 2017 Actual, 2018 to 2020 Projected, $M

	2013A	2014A	2015A	2016A	2017A	2018P	2019P	2020P
Revenues	1,944	1,804	1,757	1,678	1,608	1,542	1,479	1,419
PBIT	(2)	(139)	(141)	(113)	(101)	(167)	(230)	(291)

Notes:

- Revenues and profits for 2013 to 2017 are actuals.

- Projections for 2018 to 2020 assume that revenues decrease in 2018, 2019 and 2020 at the same rate as the decrease from 2016 to 2017 (-4.1%) and that costs remain constant.

- The projections filed by the private conventional television groups with their most recent licence renewal applications assume a lower annual rate of revenue erosion (-1.5%) but nonetheless, anticipate significant operating losses, totaling almost $111 million in 2020.

Chapter 2

1. John Aird, *Report of the Royal Commission on Radio Broadcasting* (Ottawa: Privy Council Office, 1929), 6.

2. Aird, *Royal Commission*, 7.

3. G.E. Smith, "Imperial Radio Chain Visioned by Bennett," *Globe*, May 19, 1932.

4. *Royal Commission on National Development*. Ottawa: King's Printer, 1951. 18.

5. *Royal Commission on National Development*, 4.

6. Judy LaMarsh, 27th Parliament, 2nd Session. November 1, 1967.

7. Pierre Juneau, personal conversation with author, 1984.

8. L. Brown, "Canadian Policy on Border TV Brings a Protest by 12 Senators," *New York Times*, July 16, 1975.

9. J. King, "Canada, U.S. Meet to Discuss Cable TV Commercial Deletion," *Globe and Mail*, January 14, 1976.

10. King, "Canada, U.S. Meet."

11. I. Rodger, "Pelletier Ridicules U.S. Threat to Jam TV Signals in Ontario," *Globe and Mail*, June 18, 1975.

12. R. Trumbull, "Canada Likes U.S. TV – Without Ads," *New York Times*, November 2, 1975.

13. R. Trumbull, "U.S. and Canada Stress Harmony," *New York Times*, December 18, 1975.

Chapter 3

1. Hélène Prévost, "The Baie Comeau Policy and Foreign Ownership in the Canadian Book Publishing Industry: Culture, Continentalism and Canada-U.S. Relations," (master's thesis, Carleton University, 1994), https://curve.carleton.ca/079cc849-1480-46b4-ad8b-5bd45741921e.

2. The Canada – U.S. Free Trade Agreement, Article 1607.4, 238.

3. Marci McDonald, *Yankee Doodle Dandy: Brian Mulroney and the American Agenda* (Toronto: Stoddart Publishing, 1995), 160.

4. McDonald, *Yankee Doodle Dandy*.

5. Margaret Atwood, "We need an informed debate on free trade: Just what are we getting into?" *Globe and Mail*, November 5, 1987.

6. F. MacDonald, Minister's Speech, Toronto, July 17, 1986

7. Allan Gotlieb, diplomatic cable, December 2, 1986

8. Correspondence between Flora MacDonald and her colleagues, 1986.

9. Canadian Embassy–Washington, diplomatic cable, March 4, 1987.

10. McDonald, *Yankee Doodle Dandy*, 169.

11. McDonald, *Yankee Doodle Dandy*, 187.

12. Robert Armstrong, *Broadcasting Policy in Canada* (Toronto: University of Toronto Press. 2016).

13. J. Kinsman, personal conversation with author, July 1, 2018.

14. McDonald, *Yankee Doodle Dandy*, 191.

Chapter 4

1. CRTC, *Broadcasting Policy Monitoring Report 2001* (Ottawa: CRTC, 2001).

2. CRTC, *Broadcasting Policy Monitoring Report 2001*; Telefilm Canada, *1999–2000 Annual Report* (Montreal: Telefilm Canada), https://telefilm.ca/wp-content/uploads/2016/08/telefilm-annualreport-1999-2000.pdf.

3. Canadian Heritage, Office of the Chief Audit and Evaluation Executive, *Summative Evaluation of the Canadian Film or Video Tax Credit (CPTC) / Office of the Chief Audit and Evaluation Executive, Evaluation Services Directorate* (Gatineau, Que.: Canadian Heritage, 2008).

4. CRTC, "Broadcasting Regulatory Policy CRTC 2010-167," March 22, 2010, https://crtc.gc.ca/eng/archive/2010/2010-167.htm.

5. CRTC, *Broadcasting Policy Monitoring Report 2001*.

6. CRTC, *Television Statistical and Financial Summaries, 2000–2004*; CRTC, *Pay and Specialty Statistical and Financial Summaries, 2000–2004*. Reports on file with Armstrong Consulting and originally published on the CRTC website.

7. Statistics Canada, "Newspaper Publishers, Summary Statistics, Inactive: Table 21-10-0043-01" (archived), last modified January 10, 2019, www150.statcan.gc.ca/t1/tbl1/en/tv.action?pid=2110004301.

8. CRTC, "Decision CRTC 2000-747" (archived), https://crtc.gc.ca/eng/archive/2000/db2000-747.htm.

9. CRTC, "Broadcasting Decision CRTC 2007-165" (archived), last modified June 6, 2007, https://crtc.gc.ca/eng/archive/2007/db2007-165.htm.

10. CRTC, "Broadcasting Decision CRTC 2007-429" (archived), last modified December 20, 2007, https://crtc.gc.ca/eng/archive/2007/db2007-429.htm.

11. For a detailed evaluation see: Marlene Catterall, *Scripts, Screens and Audiences: A New Feature Film Policy for the 21st Century, Report of the Standing Committee on Canadian Heritage* (Ottawa: Standing Committee on Canadian Heritage, November 2005), www.ourcommons.ca/Content/Committee/381/CHPC/Reports/RP2134619/chpcrp19/chpcrp19-e.pdf.

Chapter 5

1. Robert Benzie, Bruce Campion-Smith, and Les Whittington, "Ordinary Folks Don't Care about the Arts: Harper," *Toronto Star*, September 24, 2008.

2. Joanna Smith, "Yann Martel Shuts Down Harper Book Club," *Toronto Star*, February 1, 2011.

3. Richard Helm, "Writer Yann Martel Gives up on Mission to Bring Literature to Stephen Harper," *National Post*, February 1, 2011, https://nationalpost.com/afterword/writer-yann-martel-gives-up-on-mission-to-bring-literature-to-stephen-harper.

4. Alain Saulnier, *Ici était Radio-Canada* (Montreal: Boréal, 2014), 212.

5. Saulnier, *Ici était Radio-Canada*, 229.

6. CRTC, "Public Notice CRTC 1999-197" last modified February 22, 2012, https://crtc.gc.ca/eng/archive/1999/pb99-117.htm.

7. ThinkTV, "Net Advertising Volume."

8. Emil Protalinsky, "With 94 Billion Installs in 2017, Google Helps Android Developers Shrink Their Apps ," *Venture Beat*, May 8, 2018, https://venturebeat.com/2018/05/08/with-94-billion-installs-in-2017-google-helps-android-developers-shrink-their-apps/.

9. ThinkTV, "Net Advertising Volume."

10. CRTC, "Broadcasting Regulatory Policy CRTC 2009-329" (archived), last modified June 4, 2009, https://crtc.gc.ca/eng/archive/2009/2009-329.htm.

11. CRTC, "Broadcasting Decision CRTC 2010-782" (archived), last modified October 22, 2010, https://crtc.gc.ca/eng/archive/2010/2010-782.htm.

12. Gordon Pitts, "With $2-Billion Deal for Canwest, Shaw Wins Battle of Media Titans," *Globe and Mail*, May 3, 2010, www.theglobeandmail.com/report-on-business/with-2-billion-deal-for-canwest-shaw-wins-battle-of-media-titans/article1320806/.

13. CRTC, "Broadcasting Decision CRTC 2011-163" (archived), last modified March 7, 2011, https://crtc.gc.ca/eng/archive/2011/2011-163.htm.

14. Bell Canada Enterprises, *BCE Inc. 2010 Annual Report*, www.bce.ca/annual-reports/2010-annual-report

15. CRTC, "Broadcasting Decision CRTC 2013-310" (archived), last modified June 27, 2013, https://crtc.gc.ca/eng/archive/2013/2013-310.htm.

16. Joel Baglole, "Netflix Surges in Canada As Traditional TV Subscriptions Continue to Decline," *BayStreet.ca*, April 18, 2018.

17. "Netflix is Moving Television beyond Time-Slots and National Markets," *Economist*, June 28, 2018, www.economist.com/briefing/2018/06/30/netflix-is-moving-television-beyond-time-slots-and-national-markets.

18. CRTC, *Conventional Television, Statistical and Financial Summaries, 2013 to 2017*; CRTC, *Discretionary and On Demand Services, Statistical and Financial Summaries, 2013–2017*. These reports are available on the CRTC website: open.canada.ca/data/en/dataset/5032ef1f-bc28-4e8d-8a96-9eed77f29d99. (See Table 13.)

Table 13: Program Expenditures by Canadian Broadcasters, 2017, $

	Canadian	Foreign	Total
Private Conventional	618,249,598	599,099,591	1,217,349,189
CBC Conventional	508,592,457	19,678,877	528,271,334
Discretionary and On Demand	1,746,741,227	510,269,087	2,257,010,314
Total	2,873,583,282	1,129,047,555	4,002,630,837

Notes:

- Data on foreign program expenditures by pay and on-demand services are not available.

19. Alex Weprin, "Amazon Expected to Spend $5 Billion on Video Content this Year," *DigitalNewsDaily*, February 23, 2018, www.mediapost.com/publications/article/315055/amazon-expected-to-spend-5-billion-on-video-conte.html.

20. CRTC, "Broadcasting Order CRTC 2012-409" last modified July 26, 2012, https://crtc.gc.ca/eng/archive/2012/2012-409.htm.

21. Kate Taylor, "CRTC Chairman Jean-Pierre Blais Plays Superhero — And Villain," *Globe and Mail*, December 23, 2016, www.theglobeandmail.com/arts/television/crtc-chairman-jean-pierre-blais-plays-superhero-and-villain/article33422701/.

22. *Broadcasting Act*, 5(1), 1991.

23. Governor General David Johnston, Speech from the Throne, October 16, 2013.

24. Canada Media Fund, *2016–2017 Annual Report*, https://ar-ra16-17.cmf-fmc.ca/.

25. CRTC, "Broadcasting Regulatory Policy CRTC 2015-86" last modified March 12, 2015, https://crtc.gc.ca/eng/archive/2015/2015-86.htm.

26. Patrick O'Rourke, "Bell Says CraveTV Now Has Over 1.3 Million
    Subscribers," *Mobile Syrup*, February 8, 2018, https://mobilesyrup.
    com/2018/02/08/bell-cravetv-1-3-million-subscribers/.

27. Edmund Lee and John Koblin, "HBO Must Get Bigger and Broader,
    Says Its New Overseer," *New York Times*, July 8, 2018, www.nytimes.
    com/2018/07/08/business/media/hbo-att-merger.html.

28. "Google's Revenue Worldwide from 2002 to 2017 (in Billion U.S.
    Dollars)," *Statista*, www.statista.com/statistics/266206/googles-annual-
    global-revenue/.

29. "Search Engine Market Share Worldwide," *Statcounter Global Stats*, June
    2018, http://gs.statcounter.com/search-engine-market-share#monthly-
    201806-201806-bar.

30. "Facebook's Annual Revenue and Net Income from 2007 to 2017 (in
    Million U.S. Dollars)," *Statista*, www.statista.com/statistics/277229/
    facebooks-annual-revenue-and-net-income/.

31. "Social Media Stats Worldwide," *Statcounter Global Stats*, June 2018, http://
    gs.statcounter.com/social-media-stats#monthly-201806-201806-bar.

32. "Data Suggests Surprising Shift: Duopoly Not All-Powerful," *eMarketer*,
    March 19, 2018, www.emarketer.com/content/google-and-facebook-s-
    digital-dominance-fading-as-rivals-share-grows; Felix Richter, "25 Percent
    of Global Ad Spend Goes to Google or Facebook," *Statista*, December 7,
    2017, www.statista.com/chart/12179/google-and-facebook-share-of-ad-
    revenue/.

33. Rose Behar, "Netflix Viewing Tops Canada's Largest Stations in English
    Language Market," *Mobile Syrup*, June 1, 2018, https://mobilesyrup.
    com/2018/06/01/netflix-spotify-cancon-crtc-canada-2018-report/.

34. See: Armstrong Consulting, *The Economic Impact of TV Program Piracy in
    Canada*, May 11, 2018.

35. CRTC, *Conventional Television, Statistical and Financial Summaries,
    2013–2017*; CRTC, *Pay and Specialty Statistical and Financial Summaries,
    2013–2017*. These reports are available on the CRTC website: open.canada.
    ca/data/en/dataset/5032ef1f-bc28-4e8d-8a96-9eed77f29d99. (See Tables 14,
    15 and 16.)

Table 14: Total Staff, Canadian Broadcast Television, 2013 to 2017

	2013	2014	2015	2016	2017	Change #	%
Private Conventional	6,083	5,961	5,790	5,317	4,939	(1,145)	-19%
CBC Conventional	6,137	5,843	5,205	4,986	3,886	(2,251)	-37%
Discretionary/ On Demand	6,116	6,203	5,899	5,439	4,984	(1,132)	-19%
Total	18,337	18,007	16,893	15,742	13,810	(4,527)	-25%

Table 15: Program Expenditures by Private and CBC Conventional Television, 2013 to 2017, $M

		2013	2014	2015	2016	2017
Private Conventional	Canadian	605	619	653	633	618
	Foreign	732	717	656	610	599
	Total	1,337	1,336	1,309	1,244	1,217
CBC Conventional	Canadian	701	790	557	635	509
	Foreign	24	21	21	20	20
	Total	725	811	578	655	528
Total Conventional	Canadian	1,306	1,409	1,210	1,268	1,127
	Foreign	756	738	677	630	619
	Total	2,062	2,147	1,887	1,898	1,746

Table 16: Profitability of Canadian Discretionary and On Demand Services, 2013 to 2017, PBIT $M and %

	2013	2014	2015	2016	2017
$	1,082	1,023	922	929	1,050
%	26.5%	24,1%	21.5%	21.0%	24,1%

36. See Chapter 1 endnote 7.

37. Statistics Canada, "Newspaper Publishers, Summary Statistics: Table
     21-10-0191-01"; Statistics Canada, "Newspaper Publishers, Summary
     Statistics, Inactive: Table 21-10-0043-01." (See Table 17.)

Table 17: Canadian Newspapers, Salaries, Wages and Benefits, 2012 to 2016, $M					
				Change	
	2012	2014	2016	#	%
Salaries, wage & benefits	1,626	1,319	1,126	(500)	-31%

Notes

- Data in the two Statistics Canada tables cited above may not be perfectly
  comparable.

38. Postmedia, Annual Reports, 2010 to 2018, www.postmedia.com/investors/ financial-reports/annual-filings/. (See Table 18.)

Table 18: Postmedia - Financial Performance, 2009 to 2018, $000

	2009	2010	2011	2012	2013	2014	2015	2016	2017	2018
Revenues										
Print ads	740,058	696,494	573,920	514,987	445,547	375,457	404,685	466,573	373,514	308,557
Print circ	246,060	240,811	219,177	209,177	195,899	194,176	221,969	260,885	239,036	220,406
Digital	79,091	84,176	87,050	89,076	91,606	88,023	97,669	93,798	105,471	116,422
Other	33,866	31,022	18,622	18,637	18,531	16,599	25,960	39,121	36,243	30,908
Total	1,099,075	1,052,503	898,888	831,877	751,583	674,255	750,283	860,377	754,264	676,293
Op. Exp										
Compensation	480,493	468,655	368,516	348,608	321,224	281,085	293,326	358,967	302,668	241,835
Newsprint	92,688	66,487	57,423	52,628	40,902	30,770	37,015	50,591	45,905	39,120
Distribution			126,825	123,872	107,905	101,794	122,863	162,778	149,930	131,688
Production				29,989	28,270	37,671	58,908	70,787	75,057	84,050
Other	354,010	326,308	156,922	132,919	123,356	113,430	126,759	143,124	126,106	114,219
Total	927,191	861,450	709,686	688,016	621,657	564,750	638,871	786,247	699,666	610,912
EBITDA	171,884	191,053	189,202	143,861	129,926	109,505	111,412	74,130	54,598	65,381
Deprec/ Aprec	40,535	48,945	72,224	69,732	73,274	105,726	72,103	43,937	37,721	38,167
Impairments					99,983		153,043	267,700	25,758	9,400
Restruc/ Other	28,805	13,351	38,011	35,355	34,171	39,285	34,622	42,570	37,814	26,464
Op Profit	102,544	128,757	78,967	38,783	(77,502)	(35,506)	(148,356)	(280,077)	(46,695)	(8,650)
Other Exp										
Interest	98,426	77,833	72,284	65,446	61,900	61,914	69,157	72,649	32,721	27,527
Reorganization	27,756	57,692								
Other	109,365	(35,578)	18,837	11,087	14,902	10,041	84,573	7,967	(80,260)	(2,307)
Profit/loss Before tax	(131,003)	28,810	(12,154)	(37,750)	(154,304)	(107,461)	(302,086)	(360,693)	844	(33,870)

39. Torstar, Annual Reports, 2011 to 2017, www.torstar.com/html/investor-relations/Annual_Filings/Annual_Report/index.cfm. (See Table 19.)

Table 19: Torstar - Financial Performance, 2010 to 2017, $000

		2010	2011	2012	2013	2014	2015	2016	2017
Revenues	Total	1,483,768	1,548,757	1,485,744	1,308,791	858,134	786,631	685,099	615,685
Op Exp	Compensation	501,729	511,083	520,835	480,297	361,544	341,824	299,315	245,906
	Other	731,706	795,425	757,177	666,594	404,520	393,395	356,192	325,631
	Total	1,233,435	1,306,508	1,278,012	1,146,891	766,064	735,219	655,507	571,537
EBITDA		250,333	242,249	207,732	161,900	92,070	51,412	29,592	44,148
	Deprec/Amort	31,492	33,165	38,182	36,266	30,674	30,177	44,020	36,987
	Impairments			13,003	77,094	82,935	345,081	800	8,133
	Restruc/Other	32,648	19,411	17,778	37,219	22,646	30,233	45,823	17,512
Op Profit		186,193	189,673	138,769	11,321	(44,185)	(354,069)	(61,051)	(18,484)
Other Exp	Interest	24,135	16,629	8,759	17,460	4,253	2,046	3,080	2,213
	Other	(98,771)	(88,097)	(16,326)	1,474	12,859	46,022	15,804	4,241
Profit/loss before tax		260,829	261,141	146,336	(7,613)	(61,297)	(402,137)	(79,935)	(24,938)

40. Torstar, *2018 Third Quarter Report*, 2018, www.torstar.com/images/file/2018/Q3/Q3%20Report.pdf. (See Table 20.)

Table 20: Torstar, Financial Performance, 2018 Q1-Q3 vs 2017 Q1-Q3, $000

				Change	
		2017 Q1-Q2	2018 Q1-Q3	#	%
Revenues	Total	446,346	398,531	(47,815)	-10.7%
Op Exp	Compensation	194,542	168,402	(26,140)	-13.4%
	Other	242,239	218,113	(24,126)	-10.0%
	Total	436,781	386,515	(50,266)	-11.5%
EBITDA		9,565	12,016		
	Deprec/Amort	30,053	20,036		
	Restructuring/Other	11,600	11,649		
Op Profit		(32,088)	(19,669)		

41. *Shattered Mirror*, 31.

Chapter 6

1. Joan Bryden, "Liberals Outspent Conservatives by $1.2-Million in 2015 Election," *Globe and Mail*, June 20, 2016, www.theglobeandmail.com/news/politics/liberals-outspent-conservatives-by-12-million-in-2015-election/article30524115/.

2. Rebecca Joseph, "Liberal Government Spent $13.7M on Social Media Advertising since Election," *Global News*. September 26, 2017, https://globalnews.ca/news/3771105/liberals-social-media-advertising/.

3. Sean Silcoff, "Is Ottawa's 'Supercluster' Funding Initiative a Superboondoggle in the Making?" *Globe and Mail*, March 16, 2018, www.theglobeandmail.com/report-on-business/is-ottawas-supercluster-funding-intiative-a-superboondoggle-in-themaking/article38297014/.

4. Alex Bozikovic, "Google's Sidewalk Labs Signs Deal for 'Smart City' Makeover of Toronto's Waterfront," *Globe and Mail*, October 17, 2017, www.theglobeandmail.com/news/toronto/google-sidewalk-toronto-waterfront/article36612387/.

5. Robert Everett-Green, "Mélanie Joly Urges Patience on Long Road toward Cultural Policy Shakeup," *Globe and Mail*, April 28, 2017, www.theglobeandmail.com/news/politics/melanie-joly-bids-patience-as-she-marches-toward-cultural-policy-shakeup/article34854385/.

6. "Mélanie Joly Puts Internet Giants on Notice," *National Observer*, March 14, 2018, www.nationalobserver.com/2018/03/14/news/melanie-joly-puts-internet-giants-notice.

7. Vito Pilieci, "Web of Familiar Faces Connects Government with Online Giants," *Ottawa Citizen*, May 6, 2018, https://ottawacitizen.com/news/national/prior-relationships-between-lobbyists-and-senior-federal-staffers-raises-ethical-questions.

8. John Anderson, *An Over-the-Top Exemption* ([Ottawa:] Canadian Centre for Policy Alternatives. June 21, 2016), www.policyalternatives.ca/publications/reports/over-top-exemption.

9. Lee Sheppard, "How Does Apple Avoid Taxes?" *Forbes*, May 28, 2013, www.forbes.com/sites/leesheppard/2013/05/28/how-does-apple-avoid-taxes/#b8ec36420a78.

10. Sheppard, "How Does Apple Avoid Taxes?"

11. Jesse Drucker and Simon Bowers, "After a Tax Crackdown, Apple Found a New Shelter for its Profits," *New York Times*, November 6, 2017, www.nytimes.com/2017/11/06/world/apple-taxes-jersey.html.

12. Mark Scott, "Google Fined Record $2.7 Billion in E.U. Antitrust Ruling," *New York Times*, June 27, 2017, www.nytimes.com/2017/06/27/technology/eu-google-fine.html.

13. Scott, "Google Fined Record $2.7 Billion."

14. Scott, "Google Fined Record $2.7 Billion."

15. Prashant Rao, "Trump Bashes E.U. Over $5.1 Billion Fine for Google," *New York Times*, July 19, 2018, www.nytimes.com/2018/07/19/business/trump-eu-google.html.

16. Charles Duhigg, "The Case against Google," *New York Times Magazine*, February 20, 2018, www.nytimes.com/2018/02/20/magazine/the-case-against-google.html.

17. Duhigg, "The Case against Google."

18. Duhigg, "The Case against Google."

19. Duhigg, "The Case against Google."

20. Robert-Jan Bartunek, "EU Fines Facebook 110 Million Euros over WhatsApp Deal," *Reuters*, May 18, 2017, www.reuters.com/article/us-eu-facebook-antitrust/eu-fines-facebook-110-million-euros-over-whatsapp-deal-idUSKCN18E0LA.

21. Michael Higgins, "The U.K. Firm That Took 'Fake News to the Next Level' Using Private Information from 50M Facebook Profiles," *National Post*, March 19, 2018, https://nationalpost.com/news/world/the-u-k-firm-that-took-fake-news-to-the-next-level-using-private-information-from-50m-facebook-profiles.

22. Adam Satariano and Sheera Frenkel, "Facebook Fined in U.K. over Cambridge Analytica Leak," *New York Times*, July 10, 2018, www.nytimes.com/2018/07/10/technology/facebook-fined-cambridge-analytica-britain.html.

23. Carole Cadwalladr, "A Withering Verdict: MPs Report on Zuckerberg, Russia and Cambridge Analytica," *Guardian*, July 28, 2018, www.theguardian.com/technology/2018/jul/28/dcms-report-fake-news-disinformation-brexit-facebook-russia.

24. Patrick Greenfield, "Social Media Firms Failing to Protect Young People, Survey Finds," *Guardian*, February 26, 2018, www.theguardian.com/society/2018/feb/26/social-media-firms-failing-to-protect-young-people-survey-finds.

25. Greenfield, "Social Media Firms Failing."

26. Zeynep Tufekci, "YouTube, the Great Radicalizer," *New York Times*, March 10, 2018, www.nytimes.com/2018/03/10/opinion/sunday/youtube-politics-radical.html.

27. Amanda Taub and Max Fisher, "Where Countries are Tinderboxes and

Facebook is the Match," *New York Times*, April 21, 2018, www.nytimes. com/2018/04/21/world/asia/facebook-sri-lanka-riots.html.

28. Tamsin McMahon, "The Long Road to Fixing Facebook," *Globe and Mail*, March 9, 2018, www.theglobeandmail.com/technology/the-long-road-to-fixingfacebook/article38268627/.

29. CRTC, *Harnessing Change*.

30. Lauren Gambino, "Mark Warner: The Tech-Savvy Senator Taking Silicon Valley to Task," *Guardian*, October 31, 2017, www.theguardian.com/ us-news/2017/oct/31/mark-warner-silicon-valley-regulation-honest-ads-act.

31. "Netflix is Moving Television beyond Time-Slots and National Markets," *Economist*, June 28, 2018.

32. Todd Spangler, "Netflix, Amazon Would Be Forced to Maintain 30 per cent European Content Quotas Under Proposed EU Law," *Variety*, April 26, 2018, https://variety.com/2018/digital/global/netflix-amazon-european-content-quota-30-percent-law-1202788631/.

33. European Union, "Audiovisual Media Services Directive" last modified November 9, 2018, https://ec.europa.eu/digital-single-market/en/policies/ audiovisual-media-servicesun.

34. EU, "Audiovisual Media Services Directive."

35. Stuart Thomson, "Canadian Company Linked to Facebook Data Breach Fires Back, Accuses Critics of Wild Speculation," *National Post*, June 12, 2018, https://nationalpost.com/news/politics/canadian-company-linked-to-facebook-data-breach-fires-back-accuses-critics-of-wild-speculation.

36. Andy Blatchford, "Liberals Awarded $100,000 Contract to Man at Centre of Facebook Data Controversy," *CBC*, March 21, 2018, www.cbc.ca/ news/politics/christopher-wylie-facebook-liberals-canada-cambridge-analytica-1.4586046.

37. McMahon, "The Long Road to Fixing Facebook."

38. Daniel Leblanc, "Facebook Canada Contracts Independent Fact Checkers to Combat 'Fake News,'" *Globe and Mail*, June 27, 2018, https://www. theglobeandmail.com/politics/article-facebook-canada-contracts-independent-fact-checkers-to-combat-fake/.

39. Guillaume Bourgault-Côté, "Ottawa hausse le ton face aux géants du Web," *Le Devoir*, March 14, 2018, www.ledevoir.com/politique/canada/522578/ melanie-joly-face-aux-geants-du-web.

40. Bourgault-Côté, "Ottawa hausse le ton face aux géants du Web."

41. Leblanc, "Facebook Canada Contracts Independent Fact Checkers."

42. CRTC, *Harnessing Change*.

Chapter 7

1. Canadian Media Producers Association (CMPA), *Profile 2017: Economic Report on the Screen-based Media Production Industry in Canada*. (Ottawa: CMPA, 2017);Canadian Heritage, "Federal Tax Credit Programs for the Film and Television Production Industry," January 2015, slideplayer.com/slide/4012086/. Calculations provided by Armstrong Consulting. (See Table 21.)

Table 21: Volume of Foreign Location and Service Production, Film or Video Production Services Tax Credit, 2008 to 2017

	2008	2009	2010	2011	2012	2013	2014	2015	2016	2017
Total Volume ($M CD)	2,038	1,625	1,692	2,066	1,807	1,836	1,910	2,666	2,681	3,757
Est. PSTC ($M)	129	103	107	131	114	116	121	169	169	238
$1US=$CDN	1.03	1.11	1.08	1.03	1.01	1.01	1.03	1.09	1.22	1.25
Total Volume ($M US)	1,979	1,464	1,567	2,006	1,789	1,818	1,854	2,446	2,190	3,006
Exchg Adv/ Disadv	59	161	125	60	18	18	56	220	483	751

Notes:

- The value of the PSTC is estimated to be equal to 6.3 per cent of production volume based on data in the above-noted report by Canadian Heritage.

2. *Shattered Mirror*, 88.

3. *Shattered Mirror*, 95.

4. Statistics Canada, "Periodical Publishers, Summary Statistics: Table 21-10-0053-01"; Statistics Canada, "Newspaper Publishers, Summary Statistics: Table 21-10-0191-01"; CMPA, *Profile 2017*; CRTC, "Local Programming Data – Public Hearing of January 25th 2016" last modified November 2, 2015, https://crtc.gc.ca/Broadcast/eng/HEARINGS/2015/2015_421a. htm?_ga=1.250939718.152611219.1439833063; CRTC, *Conventional Television Statistical and Financial Summaries, 2013–2017* ([Ottawa:] CRTC, 2017), https://applications.crtc.gc.ca/OpenData/CASP/ Financial%20Broadcasting%20Summaries/Books%202017/OTA/2017%20 Conventional%20Television_Statistical%20and%20Financial%20 Summaries.pdf; CRTC, *Discretionary and On Demand, Statistical and Financial Summaries, 2013-2017, open.canada.ca/data/en/dataset/5032ef1f-bc28-4e8d-8a96-9eed77f29d99*. Calculations provided by Armstrong Consulting. (See Table 22.)

Table 22: Estimated Tax Credits for News, Newspapers, Magazines and TV News, 2017 $M

	Newspapers		Magazines		TV News	Total	
	Low	High	Low	High	Estimate	Low	High
Eligible Labour Costs	$318	$477	$162	$243	$451	$931	$1,171
Overhead	$45	$67	$23	$34	$84	$151	$185
Journalism Production Cost	$363	$544	$185	$277	$536	$1,083	$1,357
Federal Tax Credits (20%)	$73	$109	$37	$55	$107	$217	$271
Current Fed Govt Funding			$75	$75		$75	$75
Net Cost to Fed Govt	$73	$109	$(38)	$(20)	$107	$142	$196
Provincial Tax Credits (17%)	$62	$92	$31	$47	$91	$184	$231
Current Prov Govt Funding							
Net Cost to Prov Govt	$62	$92	$31	$47	$91	$184	$231
Total Tax Credits (73%)	$134	$201	$68	$102	$198	$401	$502
Current Govt Funding			$75	$75		$75	$75
Net Cost to Govt	$134	$201		$27	$198	$326	$427

Notes:

- The eligible labour costs in this table are estimates of the salaries and other compensation costs for editors, journalists, photographers, camera operators, design and layout artists and other personnel directly involved in the production of news content, excluding the labour costs associated with printing, marketing and distribution.

- Based on consultations with newspaper and magazine publishers, eligible newspaper labour costs are assumed to range from 10 per cent (low scenario) to 15 per cent (high scenario) of operating revenues. Eligible labour costs for television news are set at 75 per cent of total reported news expenses. That percentage is based on local news programming data provided to the CRTC by private television broadcasters for the 2014/15 broadcast year.

- Operating revenues for newspapers and magazines are for the most recently available year — 2016 and 2015 respectively. News expenses for television are based on the most recently available data from the CRTC — 2017.

- Overhead costs included in the eligible journalism production costs are set at 14 per cent of eligible labour costs, which is comparable to the overhead allocation for film and television production.

- The federal tax credit is set at 20 per cent of eligible labour costs equal to the combined percentage of total Canadian film and television production accounted by federal tax credits (10 per cent) and funding from the CMF/ Telefilm (10 per cent) in 2017.

- The provincial tax credit is set at 17 per cent equal to the percentage of total Canadian film and television production accounted for by provincial tax credits in 2017.

- The cost to the federal government assumes that it provides tax credits comparable to the combined federal and provincial tax credits plus CMF/ Telefilm funding, net of the funding that is currently available to Canadian periodicals through the Canadian Periodical Fund ($75 million).

5. ThinkTV, "Net Advertising Volume"; CRTC, *Communications Monitoring Report 2017*; Bree Rody-Mantha, "Canada to Fall Out of Top 10 Ad-Spend Markets by 2019: Report," *Media in Canada*, March 29, 2017, http:// mediaincanada.com/2017/03/29/canada-to-fall-out-of-top-10-ad-spend-markets-by-2019-report/; Bree Rody-Mantha, "Growth in Canadian Ad Spend to Slow across Most Media: Study," April 13, 2017, http:// mediaincanada.com/2017/04/13/growth-in-canadian-ad-spend-to-slow-across-most-media-study/; MTM, cited in "Market Insights" in *Harnessing Change*, CRTC, 2018. Calculations provided by Armstrong Consulting. (See Table 23.)

Table 23: Estimated Revenues from the Application of HST to Foreign OTTs and to the Purchase of Advertising on Foreign Digital Media, 2020, $M

Foreign OTTs	Revenues	2,010
	Federal HST (5%)	101
	Provincial HST (8%)	161
	Total HST	261
Internet ad expenditures on foreign services	Revenues	5,230
	Federal HST (5%)	262
	Provincial HST (8%)	418
	Total HST	680
Total	Federal HST (5%)	362
	Provincial HST (8%)	579
	Total HST	941

Notes:

- The provincial sales tax rate is assumed to average 8 per cent across the country.

- Estimated foreign OTT revenues in 2020 assume that the Netflix service in Canada has reached maturity, with four additional foreign OTTs in Canada (Amazon, Hulu, CBS All Access and Disney) with a growth trajectory similar to that achieved by Netflix.

- Estimated ad expenditures on foreign digital media assume that these services capture 72 per cent of total Internet advertising in Canada, as was the case in 2016, that the Internet ad market accounts for 50 per cent of total ad expenditures in Canada as was the case in 2017 and that the total ad market grows by 2.2 per cent per year.

- HST charged by foreign digital media on ad sales would be eligible for input tax credits for the purchasers and as such, may not result in an increase in HST revenues to the federal treasury.

6. Arthur Donner, *The Financial Impacts of Section 19.1 of the Income Tax Act (Bill C-58) and Simultaneous Substitution* ([Ottawa:] Communications Canada, 1990). Calculations provided by Armstrong Consulting. (See Table 24.)

Table 24: Estimated Impact of extending section 19.1 of the *Income Tax Act* to Advertising on Foreign Digital Media, 2020, $M

Estimated Internet Advertising Revenues		7,264
		Ad revenues to
	Market Share	Foreign Digital Media
Share to Foreign Digital Media	72%	5,230
	Repatriation %	Reparriated Ad Revenues
Repatriated Ad Revenues to Canadian Media	25.4%	1,330
	Ineligible Ad	Incremental
	Expenditures	Corporate Tax Revenues
Incremental Federal Corporate Tax Revenues with repatriation	3,923	585
Incremental Federal Corporate Tax Revenues w/o repatriation	5,230	785

Notes:

- The repatriation rate is set at 25.4 per cent — the rate of repatriation identified in the Donner study when section 19.1 was applied to other media.

- The federal corporate tax rate is assumed to equal 15 per cent.

7. CRTC, *Harnessing Change*.

8. Foreign OTT revenues in 2019 are projected to be $1.461 billion. Thirty per cent of those revenues equals $438 million.

9. CMPA, *Profile 2017*; CRTC, Broadcasting Notice of Consultation
   CRTC 2017-428, December 5, 2017 (https://crtc.gc.ca/eng/
   archive/2017/2017-428.htm), TV Groups, Financial Projections, Group
   Licence Renewal Applications, Reconsideration. Calculations provided by
   Armstrong Consulting. (See Table 25.)

Table 25: Impact of OTT CPE Requirement on Total Volume of Canadian Film and TV Production, 2020, $M

	2017		2020		Change in Public Funding		
	$	%	$	%	Federal	Provincial	Total
Private Broadcaster Licence Fees	412	12%	317	7%			
Public Broadcaster Licence Fees	363	11%	363	8%			
Foreign OTT			438	9%			
Federal Tax Credit	341	10%	490	10%	149		
Provincial Tax Credit	571	17%	820	17%		249	
Canadian Distributors	514	16%	737	16%			
Foreign	397	12%	569	12%			
CMF	278	8%	399	8%	121		
Telefilm	69	2%	99	2%	30		
Other Public	80	2%	115	2%			
Other Private	280	8%	401	8%			
Total	3,305	100%	4,748	100%	300	249	549

Notes:

- Private television broadcaster licence fees for 2020 have been adjusted downwards from their level in 2017 to reflect the projected reduction in Canadian program spending set out in their most recent licence renewal applications.

- Public broadcaster licence fees in absolute dollars have been held constant.

- Foreign OTT contributions have been set equal to 30 per cent of their estimated previous year revenues ($1.461 billion).

- The per cent of total volume accounted for by other financing sources has been held constant at the level achieved in 2017.

10. Jon Nathanson, "The Economics of a Hit TV Show," *Priceonomics*, October
    17, 2013, https://priceonomics.com/the-economics-of-a-hit-tv-show/.

11. "Canadian Association of Broadcasters' Code of Ethics (2002)," *Canadian
    Broadcast Standards Council*, www.cbsc.ca/codes/cab-code-of-ethics/.

INDEX

#DigiCanCon, 22
21st Century Fox, 86, 129, 131, 180, 184
30 per cent rule, 152–53, 181
7 *Jours*, 173

AggregateIQ, 149, 155–56
Alain Gourd, 61, 72–73, 78, 80–81
Alain Saulnier, 112–13
Alan Plaunt, 45–46
Allan Gotlieb, 70, 74, 84–85
Allan MacEachen, 56
Alliance Atlantis, 103, 105, 119
Amanda Todd, 149–50
Amazon, 11, 20, 22, 122, 131–32, 152–153, 179, 190–191
America Online (AOL), 114
America's Got Talent, 128
Americanizing TV shows, 164
André Malraux, 82
Android, 116, 146–47
Applied Semantics, 114
Astral Media, 120
Atom Egoyan, 105

Baie-Comeau policy, 71–75, 180
    failure of, 76
Bev Oda, 110
big media companies
    collapse of, 21
Bill C-58, 55
Bill Morneau, 31, 37, 175
book market
    Canadian, 68
book policy
    Canada's, 71
British point system, 165
broadcast standards, 153
Broadcasting Act, 27, 46, 50, 113, 123, 178
Buffy Sainte-Marie, 8
bullying, 12, 143, 149–50

Cable Production Fund, 96
cable TV, 96–99, 126

    emergence of, 53
    revenues, 125, 132
Cambridge Analytica, 148–49, 155–56
Canada Council, 10, 18, 22, 27, 47, 66, 110
Canada Media Fund, 33, 49, 57, 98, 125, 180, 191, *see also* Canadian Television Fund
Canada–United States Free Trade Agreement, 60, 66, 74, 79–80, 91
Canadian Association of Broadcasters' Code of Ethics, 186
Canadian Broadcast Development Fund, 56
Canadian Cable Corporation, 51
Canadian content, 30, 31, 35, 43, 44, 48, 55, 64, 122, 159, 161–62, 165–67, 180–81, 190, 191
    30 per cent rule, 181
    definition, 49
Canadian cultural policy, 22, 27, 38, 42–44, 46, 49–50, 64 *see also Cultural Policy for the Digital Age*
Canadian culture, 19, 23, 78–79
    and US dominance, 42, 125–26
Canadian culture industry, 23
Canadian media
    golden age, 104
Canadian media advertising
    collapse of, 26
Canadian Media Fund, 98–99, 125
Canadian Radio-television and Telecommunications Commission (CRTC), 30, 51, 53, 96, 99, 113–14, 118, 120, 122–24, 126, 149, 159, 160, 178–79, 187, 198–, 209, 217–20
Canadian Television Fund, 96
Canadianness, 49
Canwest Global Communications Corp, 119
Catherine McKenna, 157
CBC
    bias against, 110–12
    Conservatives attack, 113

Chrétien Liberals, 76, 95
Citysearch, 146
Citytv, 11, 38, 99, 103, 122, 131
click ads, 117
Code of Practice on Disinformation
    European Union, 186
Comcast, 128–30, 184
Conrad Black, 101
consumer behaviour, 128
Corus, 132–33, 183–84
Crave, 127
Creative Canada Policy Framework, 27, 30
cultural garden, 13
Cultural Policy for the Digital Age, 24–25
cultural sovereignty, 62, 65–66, 70,
    78–79, 83–84, 91
cyber bullying, 150

Daniel Weinzweig, 85
David Cronenberg, 105
David Silcox, 61, 66, 69, 73–74
De Montigny Marchand, 67, 70,
    72–73, 81
Death Stars, 14, 95
democracy, 20, 156, 162, 167, 170,
    185, 188
    and fake news, 25
    and newspapers, 25
Denys Arcand, 105
Desmarais family, 33–34
digital advertising, 116, 118, 124, 134,
    145
    revenue, 130
Digital Media Exemption Order, 114,
    118, 123, 126, 178, 187
digital news incubator, 28
Digital, Culture, Media and Sport
    Committee, 149
Disney, 86, 127, 128–131, 164, 178,
    180, 18–85
    streaming service, 128
*Disruption: Change and Churning in
    Canada's Media Landscape*, 25
DoubleClick, 114
Doug Finley, 111

Ed Greenspon, 171, 173
English Canada
    cultural inferiority, 43

FAANGs, 11–13, 113, 121–22,
    124–25, 131, 141–45, 147, 154, 158,
    177, 179, 185–87, 189–90
    definition, 11
Facebook, 12, 20, 114–18, 125, 130,
    137, 140, 147–49, 152, 156–57,
    176–77, 187, 189, 198
    and Ryerson, 28
    fake news, 156
Facebook and Google dominance, 115
FairPlay coalition, 160
fake news, 12, 20, 26, 28, 143–44,
    148–52, 155, 156–58, 170, 173,
    186–87, 189, 192
Feature Film Fund, 104
Federal Bureau of Investigation, 148
Federal Communications Commission,
    54
Flashpoint, 163
Flora MacDonald, 83–85, 88–93, 104
foreign content, 44, 48, 167
foreign publishers, 68–69, 75
Fox, *see* 21st Century Fox
Frank Mancuso, 86
freedom of expression, 7, 154, 187, 191
Future of Democracy and Journalism
    Fund, 25, 170

Gerald Butts, 157
Gérard Pelletier, 54
Getty Images, 146
Golden Tree Asset Management,
    133–34
Goldman Sachs, 103
Google, 20, 25, 114, 116, 125, 145,
    186, 191, 198, *see also* Facebook and
    Google dominance
    abusive conduct, 146–47
    lobbying, 141–42
Google and Facebook ad revenue,
    130, 176
Graham Spry, 45–46
grand theory of cultural sovereignty,
    62
Greenspon, 171, 173

*Harnessing Change: The Future of
    Programming Distribution in Canada*,
    35, 159, 178